DEVELOPMENTS IN HIGH SCHOOL PSYCHOLOGY

High School Behavioral Science Series, Volume 1

Edited by
Harwood Fisher

Associate Professor of Education
Director Post Masters Training of Teachers of
High School Psychology
City College of the City University of New York

and

James M. Johnson

Associate Professor
of Psychology
State University of
New York at Plattsburgh

Judith Kaufman

Assistant Professor
of Psychology
Yeshiva University
New York

Aileen Schoeppe

Associate Professor of
Psychology
New York University

Ethel Weiss

Associate Professor of
Psychology
City College of the City
University of New York

Behavioral Publications
New York

Library of Congress Catalog Number 73-20023
ISBN: 0-87705-111-9
Copyright © 1974 by Behavioral Publications

BEHAVIORAL PUBLICATIONS
72 Fifth Avenue
New York, New York 10011

Printed in the United States of America
456789 987654321

Library of Congress Cataloging in Publication Data
Main entry under title:

Developments in high school psychology.

   Includes the proceedings of two conferences: a City College seminar on the teaching of high school psychology held Sept. 1971, and the Symposium on Problems in High School Psychology, held at City College of New York, Jan. 1972.
   1. Psychology—Study and teaching (Secondary)—Congresses. I. Fisher, Harwood, ed. [DNLM: 1. Curriculum. 2. Curriculum—Congresses. 3. Psychology—Education. 4. Psychology—Education—Congresses. BF77 D491 1974]

BF77.D45   150'.7'12   73-20023

CONTENTS

The Contributors   ix
Preface   xi

SECTION I
PROBLEMS AND ISSUES IN
HIGH SCHOOL PSYCHOLOGY

1. Overview
   A. Educational Currents in Pre-College
   Psychology   3
   Harwood Fisher
   B. Needs and Objectives in High School
   Psychology   10
   Harwood Fisher, G. Susan Gray, Ethel Weiss
   C. The Training of Pre-College Teachers
   of Psychology   15
   D. Summary and Perspective   19

2. High School Psychology: Past Trends and
   Future Hopes   23
   T. L. Engle

3. High School Psychology Courses: To Be
   or Not to Be?   45
   Richard A. Kasschau

4. A Survey of High School Psychology: Teacher
   and Course Characteristics   57
   James J. Ryan

5. A Survey of the Status of Pre-College
   Psychology in Florida: 1970-1971   95
   Robert J. Stahl and J. Doyle Casteel

6. The Chancellor Questions the Issues   113

SECTION II
PROCEEDINGS OF CONFERENCES ON
HIGH SCHOOL PSYCHOLOGY

Introduction to Workshops: Overview   119

Part I: Curriculum

7. Workshop on Curriculum: Summary and Analysis   123
   Sheldon R. Roen, Coordinator
   Aileen Schoeppe, Editor

8. High School Psychology in Practice:
   A Field Approach   149
   Ira Lipton

9. Should High School Psychology be Relevant?   155
   Ethel Weiss

Part 2: Communication with Students

10. Workshop on Communication with Adolescent
    Students   159
   Alfred Weiss, Coordinator
   Ethel Weiss, Editor

11. Communication with High School Students   173
   Margaret Miller

12. Communicating with Adolescent Students:
    An Experiential Approach   179
   Alfred Weiss

13. Editor's Analysis   187

Part 3: Teacher Training

14. Workshop on Teacher Training   191
    Harwood Fisher, Coordinator
    Ethel Weiss, Editor

15. Preparation in the Psychology of Learning for
    High School Psychology Teachers   207
    Marion R. Brown

16. Outline for a Program of Graduate Training of
    High School Psychology Teachers   221
    Harwood Fisher

Part 4: Issues in Certification

17. Certification Workshop: Summary and Analysis   231
    William Sivers, Coordinator
    James M. Johnson, Editor

18. Psychology in New York State High Schools   241
    Gordon E. Van Hooft

19. Some Procedures of Certification Relative to
    Initiating a Secondary Education Program
    in Psychology   255
    Mary Talbot Keliher

Part 5: Funded Programs

20. Workshop on Funding Programs:
    Summary and Analysis   263
    James M. Johnson, Coordinator and Editor

21. A Model of a Training Program for Secondary
    Behavioral Science Teachers   271
    James M. Johnson

Index   287

The Contributors

Marion R. Brown, Associate Professor of Education City College of the City University of New York

Doyle Casteel, Associate Professor Department of Secondary Education University of Florida

T. L. Engle, Professor Emeritus of Psychology Indiana University at Fort Wayne

H. Fisher, Associate Professor of Education City College of the City University of New York City

G. Susan Gray, Assistant Professor of Education, City College of the City University of New York

Richard Kasschau, Associate Professor of Psychology University of South Carolina

Mary Talbot Keliher, Assistant Professor of Psychology Marywood College Scranton, Pennsylvania

James M. Johnson, Associate Professor of Psychology State University of New York at Plattsburgh

Ira Lipton, Teacher of Psychology Jamaica High School, New York City

Margaret Miller, Teacher of Psychology United Nations International School New York City

James J. Ryan, Professor of Psychology University of Wisconsin at La Crosse

Aileen Schoeppe, New York University

Harvey B. Scribner, Chancellor Board of Education of New York City

William Sivers, Chief, Bureau of Psychological Services New York State Department of Education

Robert Stahl, Member of the Research Division and Teaching Staff P. K. Yonge Laboratory School College of Education, University of Florida

Alfred Weiss, Associate Professor of Education City College of the City University of New York

Ethel Weiss, Associate Professor of Psychology City College of the City University of New York

Gordon Van Hooft, Acting Director Division of School Supervision New York State Education Department

Preface

High school students of today ask *more* than "Who am I?" They ask about people: Who are people, how do they live, how do I help them, where do I fit in? The students ask these questions of the schools, questions of sociology, anthropology and psychology. The curriculum of behavioral science is increasingly demanded in the high schools. What does this mean and what problems does it raise?

In a way, the students are responding to the age of instant replay. History is now visible, recorded, and available—faster than a flashback. Time photography can unfold a flower within moments. Young people want to learn about their past, present and future. They want to know everything all at once, to know their origins, and to know that their origins are relevant to their experiences. They want to know about the future and how they can get there. The way the young people experience time is in terms of movement and change. Movement and change are in every action and every moment. The concern of the young is the evolvement and transformation of their behavior and the things they experience. The age of instant replay is an age in which history, development and even dynamics, have been technologized.

Young people want to understand their origins, their feelings, their place in society, the how and why of their development. It is no surprise that in an age of technologized facts, they turn to an analysis of behavior. Behavior is immediate. Behavior *is* a replay. Behavior can be replayed: present, past and future.

More and more young people are turning their search for understanding toward an interest in the behavioral sciences. We can be pessimistic and see this as an abandonment of traditional courses in the high schools. We can see it as a cutting off from the past, an emphasis on the superficial, a narcissistic concern with the immediate. Or we can be optimistic and see the high school student as ingenious. He is synthesizing history and science in his turn toward the study of behavior. He is forming a bridge, between the study of man's evolvement and change, and the effects of technology.

The study of behavioral sciences by the high school student typifies the intellectual and technological developments of our age. It is particularly exciting to introduce this book as a modest initial exploration of the issues that arise with the growth of behavioral science in the high schools. Who will teach the courses? Who will teach the teachers? What shall be the content? How do you communicate with the students?

This first volume directs itself to exploring these issues in psychology. Psychology in the high schools presents a great hope for communication with the student. At the same time the issues in teaching psychology in the schools are intrinsically complex. Psychology may certainly help to answer the student's questions about himself, his behavior and the behavior of other people. However, is psychology a service to the student or an academic discipline? Is it an experience or a subject area? The fact that psychology can be presented as a body of knowledge, and that it can also be a social service, presents great curricular, pedagogical and ethical issues.

The volume is meant as one which states issues and perhaps suggests some directions to be taken. The Editors feel that much work must be undertaken in this area before answers and solutions can be put forth. Other volumes in this series will review the status and the issues of sociology and anthropology in the high schools.

OVERALL PURPOSE OF THIS VOLUME

The overall purpose of this book is to present an overview of the status and the issues in the teaching of psychology in the high schools. The book is divided into two major sections.

Section One provides a broad view of psychology in the high schools with respect to the need for the subject, its educational objectives, and its current status. This section was compiled to provide the reader with background information from which to view the exploration and discussion of the specific issues in Section Two.

Section Two has been compiled to illustrate how a group of educators, teacher trainers and high school teachers of psychology are currently facing the issues and formulating the problems in teaching psychology in the high schools. Section Two is comprised of the proceedings of the City College Seminar on the teaching of high school psychology and the Symposium on Problems in High School Psychology held at City College of New York. In September 1971 a Seminar was held for the New York City high school teachers of psychology. The Seminar was sponsored by the School of Education at City College. In January 1972, the Symposium at City University was held for high school teachers of psychology, college personnel concerned with the training of these teachers, school psychologists and school personnel concerned with guidance and psychological issues. The Symposium included four workshops. These workshops and their coordinators are listed below:

Communication with the High School Student
  Alfred Weiss
  City College of the City University
  of New York

Problems in Course Curriculum
  Sheldon Roen
  Human Sciences, Inc.

The Present and Future in Teacher Training
  Harwood Fisher
  City College of the City University
  of New York

Certification Problems
  William Sivers
  Bureau of Psychological Services
  New York State Department of Education

Funding High School Programs
  James M. Johnson
  State University of New York
  at Plattsburgh

These meetings allowed discussion and exploration of problems in curriculum, teacher training, communication with students, state certification of teachers and funding of programs. In keeping with the openness of the Seminar and the Symposium, the Editors intend Section Two to indicate what some of the present thinking and growing pains are like. The section does not purport to solve issues raised in the overview in Section One. The proceedings should serve as stimulus for a series of directions to approach the problems discussed.

Harwood Fisher
School of Education
City College of the City University of New York
January 1973

Section I

Problems and Issues
in
High School Psychology

1. Overview

A. Educational Currents in Pre-College Psychology

HARWOOD FISHER

My purpose here is to present a broad overview of a series of major questions about psychology on the pre-college level. What is the need for high school teaching of psychology? Who is the high school psychology teacher now, and who will he be in the future? How can this person be best trained; what sorts of training programs exist and can be developed? What are the student's as well as the teacher's needs and perceptions relative to curriculum development?

One begins to search the question of need in basic terms. Whose need? One teaches psychology to the secondary school student, if *he* needs it. This question recalls the medieval image of the man with one eye turned upward and the other turned downward. In our time, this image seems to capture symbolically the inner tension of the adolescent. The high school student seems to look upward with one eye, toward his aspirations, and down-

Portions of this paper were presented at the two conferences summarized in this book: (*a*) Seminar on the Teaching of High School Psychology, New York, City College, September 1971 and (*b*) Symposium on Problems in High School Psychology, City College of the City University, New York, January 1972.

ward with the other, toward his despair. At the same time he cannot look forward. He cannot look straightforward at his personal and social reality and take in all he might in his high school education.

At no other time in history would it be as necessary to focus upon the needs of the adolescent himself in order to provide information about how he is growing, information about his changing body and information about his relations with other people. I am reminded of the Inhelder and Piaget (1958) description of tremendous intellectual growth during adolescent years. High school teachers certainly notice that irrespective of how the student expresses himself, he is full of ideas and intellectual curiosity. At the same time the student may buckle under the demands of his bodily urges and his need to extend his social roles and vistas.

High school psychology is needed if it can answer the questions of the adolescent students' condition. The major question in the teaching of high school psychology is this: how can we help the high school student understand and integrate his educational exposure along with his intellectual, physical, and social urges? Further, who is the teacher who can do this, and even more cogently, who is likely to be teaching a course in high school psychology? It is a general problem, at present, in the behavioral sciences that the high school teacher will have been trained in some discipline other than that he will be teaching. It certainly may be that the teacher of high school psychology, to a certain extent, is going to teach from the point of view of his own previous discipline.

Our own educational background determines how we approach the problem of teaching the adolescent how to understand himself. For example, if the problems of the high school student would be addressed by a lawyer, the lawyer might take up an issue of responsibility in society or the foundations of the individual's place in society in relation to sanctions. If these same problems are taken up by a hygiene teacher, we might gain information about the physical aspects of sexual growth and behavior. Similarly, we can see how a priest or a poet might attack these problems: the priest might begin with a rationalist's notion of order and then apply it to individual phenomena; the poet might begin with a romantic reverence for the particular, and then lead one to a notion of order. In any case, the priest might offer an ordered way of understanding growth and change, and the poet might talk about and try to offer joy in the experience of growth.

How does the de facto psychology teacher address himself to the needs of the high school student? Recently I talked with a number of New York City social studies teachers who are currently teaching psychology, and I learned about some of their teaching aims (Fisher, 1971). Three major objectives seemed to emerge from our discussion:

1. To teach pupils to be aware of themselves.
2. To teach pupils to communicate with peers. (This objective should serve to teach the student that there are others "in the same boat" and that he can talk to them.)
3. To teach the student ways to think about social problems. (This objective should serve to teach pupils to form hypotheses and to know that there is a scientific approach to social issues.)

In order to evaluate these objectives we must continue along our pragmatic line and ask: who the teachers are and whether they can achieve the goals. The teachers with whom I spoke were New York City teachers. In New York

State, the high school teacher of psychology is now typically the social studies teacher. That is, certification is generic, and psychology is regarded as a social studies alternative. Does the background and training of the typical social studies teacher enable him to achieve these objectives? Of course there is no easy answer to this question, but at present perhaps the question can be raised in terms of the psychological background of the typical high school psychology teacher, and the responsibilities of the graduate schools in providing programs.

The thinking of the teachers questioned suggested that the major content of a secondary school course in psychology, focus on the adolescent students' growth. The implication is that the goal of facilitating adolescent growth is met directly by teaching pupils self and social awareness and by teaching them about the problems involved in adolescent growth. In this view, the content of the psychology course and its objectives may be one and the same. While we shall discuss this view in some detail later (Chapter 13) a brief comment is made here: education involves a two-step process. One learns content A, in order to do B. One learns to be a psychologist in a certain way first, and then learns to translate this into a way of helping the adolescent student. This might sound platitudinous were it not for the deep problems that appear to arise, because of the lack of knowledge of psychology on the part of many teachers who are asked to teach the course in the secondary schools. As a matter of fact, this lack of knowledge expresses itself in the teacher's anxieties. For example, high school psychology teachers in New York City show great concern over the limitations of the classroom as a place for personal and social dynamics, as a place for quasi-therapeutic approaches and as a place for encounter tactics. The concern is expressed in terms of ethics, teacher competency and knowledge of what to do rather than in terms of student goals. There is general agreement about the goals, but not on the topics the teacher is prepared to teach and methods of teaching them.

With increasing teacher knowledge of psychological issues, there may be less of a tendency to narrow the curriculum. The question of who the psychology teacher *should* be is intimately tied to what he knows, what the students want to know, and the teacher's ability to form appropriate and reachable goals.

Margaret Miller at the United Nations School in New York City, (1971) Kasschau at South Carolina (1971), and others have pointed to the broad interests of the adolescent students in problems in psychology. Problems that stimulate student interest appear in such areas as animal psychology, (especially if one gives students animals to work with) learning, social psychology and the psychology of achievement. Students are very interested in questions about how one achieves, how achievement is measured and how achievement can be measured in a valid way. These latter questions ultimately may lead the student to more general issues of psychological measurement. Moreover, one of the major areas of interest in psychology for both teachers and students is motivation. The experience of teachers on a national level, as I understand it, seems to bear out the view that students want information about the *foundation* areas in psychology.

What are the consequents of the absence of the teacher's knowledge about foundations of psychology? Perhaps this lack of information produces an over-reliance on the teacher's part upon the dynamics of behavior, rather than upon substantive information. In the schools the expert in the area of personality dynamics would be the school psychologist. He would be the individual to pursue the therapeutic approach in relation to adolescent problems. The goals of the school psychologist and the high school teacher of psychology have significant overlap in the area of their concern over the problems of the adolescent and his coming of age. However, the approaches to these problems should come from different directions: the approach of the classroom teacher should be from more of a substantive, factual direction, while that of the school psychologist should be from an interpersonal, therapeutic base.

For the most part the current teacher of psychology is prepared in social studies and has strong ties in the social science area. In reality, there is no reason that a psychology course could not better be taught by a biology teacher, or indeed by a lawyer, priest or poet. Edwin Boring pointed to the fact that great psychologists are often people who prepare first in another discipline. His position was that it really did not matter in what area you prepared as long as your preparation was good. One can think of many examples: Ernst Schachtel, a lawyer, made a contribution to psychoanalysis; Freud, a neurologist, made outstanding contributions to the field of psychology; and Piaget, the epistemologist, makes very influential contributions to child psychology. There *is* an identity crisis when those of us who come from different fields enter the field of psychology. The contention I have in terms of meeting this crisis is that there will be anxiety regarding perceived lacks or gaps of information about specific areas of psychology. This anxiety can be reduced as the psychology teacher develops competencies in these areas, and as he feels specific mastery in the areas of

learning, social psychology, motivation and measurement
— the so-called *foundation* areas.

Prior to discussing what is currently being done and
what is projected at City College in the School of Education with regard to the training of pre-college psychology teachers, it would be helpful to consider, from
a historical perspective what has been done across the
nation in the teaching of psychology to high school
students.

B. Needs and Objectives in High School Psychology

HARWOOD FISHER, G. SUSAN GRAY AND ETHEL WEISS[1]

A brief review of the status of high school psychology's objectives will be offered here as an overview. More specific reviews of the status of high school psychology appear in the papers to follow in Section I. (See especially Engle, Chapter 2, and the Stahl and Casteel bibliography, Chapter 5.)

Psychology has been offered as a course in secondary schools for over a hundred years (Nebergall, 1965). In recent years, there has been an increase in the number of high schools offering psychology as an elective course to students. In 1965, 49 of the 50 states included a course of psychology as part of their high school curriculum, although only 1.4 percent of the total number of students attending the high schools which offered psychology actually were enrolled in a psychology course (Thornton, 1965). In 1970, 60 percent of California high schools offered a course in psychology (Parrott, 1970). In New York State, out of 792 school districts 66 offered psychology at the secondary school level in 1971 (K. Pomeroy, personal communication, 1971). Additional evidence for an increase in the practice of teaching

[1] The assistance of Bernard Hammer, Ph.D., and Norman Shapiro, Ph.D., is gratefully acknowledged.

psychology at the pre-college level comes from data collected in South Carolina, where there was a 19 percent increase in the number of student-semester hours of psychology taught in South Carolina high schools from 1969-1970 to the 1970-1971 academic year (Kasschau, 1971).

Although there is a long history of teaching psychology in secondary schools, the history has been marked with a lack of consensus on the part of high school educators, university educators and professional psychologists about the objectives of a high school level course. In addition, there has been no concerted effort to systematically analyze and identify desired objectives of a high school psychology course concomitant with the increased im-plementation of psychology courses at the secondary school level. Kremer (1968) studied the objectives, course content and preparation of high school psychology teach-ers in Oregon. He found that the desired goals and objectives of a high school psychology course, as stated by high school teachers of psychology, did not coincide with the objectives stated by 130 teachers of psychology in other states, the objectives expressed by a group of psychologists, or the objectives stressed by the Oregon Department of Education. The Oregon teachers stressed learning, family living and philosophy of life as important course topics, whereas the other three groups emphasized the scientific basis of psychology as desirable course content. The tendency of university-level educators and psychologists to stress the scientific foundation of psychol-ogy, while high school teachers stress personality, and personal and social adjustment as course objectives has been demonstrated in other survey studies (McNeely, 1958; Noland, 1966; Thornton, 1965). After evaluating material used in teaching psychology at the high school level, a team of investigators at Oberlin College recommended to the American Psychological Association (APA) that a standardized course in psychology be developed for use in the high schools (Final Report, Oberlin College, 1970). At present such a plan for development is under way by APA, subject to appropriate funding (APA *Monitor,* October 1971).

Attitudes of high school and university educators toward the practice of teaching psychology in high schools reflects, to a certain extent, the lack of agreement of the two groups about desired course objectives and goals. Noland (1966) surveyed high school educators and psychologists in Ohio and found that 90 percent of the high school educators favored teaching psychology at the secondary school level, while only 60 percent of university psychologists reacted favorably to the practice. Because of the notable lack of attitudinal survey studies, it is impossible to determine if attitudes toward teaching psychology in high schools on the part of high school and university educators have changed in recent years, or, if there has been little change in attitudes, why university-level psychologists react less positively to a secondary school course in psychology.

Two characteristics of existing high school psychology programs have contributed to the lack of consistency of course content and quality from school to school and from state to state. Although there is wide agreement that high school teachers of psychology are enthusiastic about their courses (Hansen, 1964; McNeely, 1958), there is also wide agreement that these teachers are often poorly prepared to teach psychology. Noland (1966) found that high school teachers of psychology in Ohio were not adequately trained in their knowledge of the field. Many of the teachers had majored in social studies, English, or physical education in college, with only a minor in psychology. Similar conclusions were drawn by Nebergall (1965), who found that many high school psychology teachers relied heavily on the textbook they used to determine course content. Goodale (1970) discovered that in Michigan, Pennsylvania and New York, the majority of high school psychology teachers did not major in psychology in college. As determined by Kasschau (1971), the average teacher of psychology in the high school has had between 8 and 13 credit hours in psychology at the undergraduate level.

Not only is there a need for more thorough training of high school teachers of psychology, but there is also a need for course textbooks and materials specifically designed for use in teaching psychology at the pre-college level. According to Thornton (1966), there are only six textbooks used in high school psychology courses which were created specifically for use at this level. In addition, the emphases of these books were placed on personality and interpersonal relations, mental hygiene, and the biological foundations of psychology, which may be the reason that these topics are most frequently cited by high school psychology teachers as desirable course content. Nebergall's survey determined that there are very few psychology texts suitable for use in the high schools, and Noland (1966) also stressed the need for a consistent, integrated treatment of psychological topics in textbooks to be used in the high schools.

In summarizing the research concerned with the teaching of psychology at the high school level, the following conclusions may be made:

1. There is a need to systematically identify desired course objectives and goals for a high school psychology course in an effort to insure some sort of consistency and standardization of course content across schools.

2. More needs to be known about attitudes of high school and university educators toward teaching psychology at the high school level in order to determine if there is a relationship between attitudes and expressed course objectives.
3. There is a need for programs which more adequately and thoroughly train high school teachers of psychology.
4. Textbooks and supplementary materials for use in high school psychology courses are desperately needed.

As can be seen from this brief review, there are a great many areas which require clarification and explanation in the teaching of pre-college psychology. Thus far we have discussed the needs of high school students and some of the specified objectives of high school psychology courses. Let us now turn to the training of pre-college psychology teachers.

C. The Training of
Pre-College Teachers of Psychology

The preparation of secondary school teachers of psychology has generally been haphazard and insufficient (Goodale 1970, Kremer 1968, Noland 1966; Professor Engle's discussion in Chapter 2). In addressing this issue, we may merely refer briefly to some survey findings which point up the problem: The studies referred to above seem to indicate a real lack of training in the *foundations* of psychology.: usually fewer than one-third of the teachers in a given sample are reported to have had a course in experimental psychology. The average high school psychology teacher had somewhere between 8 and 13 hours of undergraduate psychology courses. Three to six of these hours are apparently on the introductory level. This information leads to the conclusion that universities and colleges should initiate programs for the specific preparations of psychology teachers. This would be valid, notwithstanding the fact that at one level of preparation, there needs to be a focus on behavioral science in general. However, at another level of preparation, namely the post-master's level, there is a need for specific preparation and for choice within the behavioral sciences. What is needed is an articulated program in the behavioral sciences, beginning at the undergraduate level. Such a sequence is described in more detail elsewhere (Fisher, 1972); however, some general points may be made here: preparation as far as the undergraduate is concerned, needs to be specific, and while the questions of the humanistic approach to dynamics and adjustment are central, adequate attention has to be given to the "hard science components." Programs may be on two levels. Many people would like to go directly into the teaching of psychology in the high school. They would enroll in programs leading to a master's degree. Such programs should be broad-based introductions to behavioral science, including anthropology, sociology, and psychology.

In the past, City College of New York has moved in several directions which may be helpful in the graduate education of the pre-college psychology teacher. We have introduced some successful fieldwork based programs for the psychology courses in undergraduate teacher education. For example, field programs in tutoring and faculty field participation are component experiences in our undergraduate course in learning. The undergraduate fieldwork-based introduction to psychology and education has several important features for an articulated and integrated training program:

1. The fieldwork-based program may lead to a specification of teacher competence.
2. Such programs can involve both development of teacher competence in psychology, and joint faculty-student investigation of factors in the teaching process.

Some major considerations in establishing the goals of training involve the following *desiderata:* the high school psychology teacher has to be given opportunities to function within his training program, as an associate to his university counterparts. There is much to be learned from each other by the high school teacher and the the teacher trainer, relative to curriculum development and research into ways of influencing values, attitudes and growth of the adolescent student. Conjoint programming by psychology and education departments (or schools) is necessary in order that *foundation* courses can be complete, and that the issues of pedagogy may be met from an educational and psychological point of view. An appropriate training program should make it possible to face the complex issue of the psychological education for the pupil in such a way as to develop diverse curricula. Perhaps an approach along the lines of a modular technique would be effective and would enable the facing of problems, especially in urban areas with a diverse pupil body.

It may be good here to sum up these general considerations as a series of goals for a training program:

1. The foundations for the study of psychology as a behavioral science need to be included.
2. The program should be an integrated one beginning at the undergraduate and proceeding to the post-master's (and possibly doctoral) level.
3. Joint faculty-student associateships would foster research and development in curriculum pedagogy, and in the psychological investigations of the classroom and the secondary school student.
4. Teachers should be made aware that they are training future leaders in the behavioral sciences, as well as providing some psychological information which may be personally helpful to the individual pupil.
5. It is especially important to communicate to the teacher of psychology that there are ways of coordinating the teacher's work in the schools with that of the psychological services personnel.
6. An understanding of pedagogy relative to psychological services should involve knowledge of the following areas: educational psychology, psychological testing, special education, foundations of psycho-diagnosis, and psychotherapy.

7. A thorough groundwork in the study of the needs of the adolescent student must be provided.

These issues will be discussed at length in Section II of this book. General curricular issues are presented and discussed in Section II, Part 2. Part 2 develops the issue of the needs of the adolescent student and some problems in communication, while Part 3 discusses teacher training more fully, and includes an outline for graduate training. Part 5 includes a description of a program for undergraduates.

D. Summary and Perspective:
A Prospectus of the Remaining Chapters

This chapter has attempted to provide a broad overview of problems and issues in the teaching of high school psychology. Questions were raised with particular respect to the need for psychology in the high schools, the nature of the *de facto* teacher of secondary school psychology, factors in certification which affect present-day teachers and the training of these teachers, the status of the goals of high school psychology courses and the goals of a training sequence for present and future teachers.

In the ensuing papers of Section I of this volume, more perspective and search into these questions will be offered. In Chapter 2 Professor T. E. Engle provides an in-depth review of the history of high school psychology. On the basis of his own considerable activity and publication in the area he offers a series of cogent projections for the future. Professor Richard Kasschau's approach in Chapter 3 is to offer ideas relative to curriculum development by first reviewing three issues: the nature of the high school student who wants to take the course, the curriculum development efforts in other disciplines and the goals of the teaching of psychology. The reader will note that Professor Kasschau provides us with some fine detail about his own situation in South Carolina. Other papers in Section I have been chosen to provide the reader with

19

specifics that concern other geographical areas in the United States. Professor Ryan's paper (Chapter 4) provides one sample of survey data from the upper Midwest. The reader may compare his description of teacher characteristics with the Stahl and Casteel data concerning the state of Florida (Chapter 5) and with the provocative questions raised by Chancellor Scribner when addressing a symposium with a large contingent of New York City teachers (Chapter 6). Moreover, this selection of different geographic considerations may be of interest in respect to some specific issues in Section II. Many of the curricular and pedagogical concerns of Parts 1 and 2 are put forth from the point of view of New York City, New York State, and its environs. The training programs described by Professor Fisher (New York City), in Part 3, by Sister Mary Keliher (Pennsylvania) in Chapter 19 and by Professor Johnson (New York State) in Chapter 21 may be compared, in terms of the needs of teachers and the concepts of curriculum, with the different geographic considerations of Section I.

The reader may find it instructive to compare the discussion of state certification (Part 4) and the consequent effects on curriculum (see particularly Dr. Van Hooft's paper, Chapter 18) with the status quo in South Carolina and Florida (Chapters 3 and 5).

Lastly, the reader may wish to note that Professor Ryan's paper has been included as a fine example of the survey approach. It is necessary to look at developments in high school psychology by way of many different currents which determine its direction. Section I provides both a historical look at the status of psychology in the high schools as well as some informative survey approaches. Section II offers additionally an experiential view, involving the shared experiences of concerned educators.

REFERENCES

Fisher, H. Graduate training for pre-college teachers of psychology. *Psychology in the Schools,* 1972 **9,** 3, 321-325.

Fisher, H. Conference on high school psychology. Panel discussion, Executive Council of the Association of Teachers of Social Studies, New York, December 1971.

Fisher, H. The need for graduate education for pre-college teachers of psychology. Paper read at Seminar for Pre-College Psychology, New York City College, September 1971.

Goodale, R. A. A survey of high school teachers of psychology in Massachusetts. *Teaching of Psychology Newsletter,* June, 1970.

Hansen, J. H. The social studies program of a representative sample of Wisconsin junior high schools and the preparation of social studies teachers. Unpublished doctoral dissertation, University of Wisconsin, 1964.

Inhelder, B. and Piaget, J. *The growth of logical thinking from childhood to adolescence.* New York: Basic Books, 1958.

Kasschau, R. Talk presented at Symposium on Pre-College Psychology. At American Psychological Association Convention, Washington, D.C., September, 1971.

Kremer, R. J. Objectives, course content and preparation of teachers for psychology classes in Oregon High School. Doctoral dissertation, Oregon State University, 1968.

McNuly, P. R. Materials, techniques and methods in teaching psychology in Indiana secondary schools. Doctoral dissertation, Indiana University, 1958.

Nebergall, N. S. A study of the teaching of high school psychology and a proposed text plan. Doctoral dissertation, University of Oklahoma, 1965.

Noland, R. L. The Role of psychology as a secondary school subject in Ohio. Doctoral dissertation, University of Cincinnati, 1966.

Oberlin College Program on the teaching of psychology in the secondary school. Final Report, June 15-July 17, 1970.

Thornton, B. M. A national survey of the teaching of psychology in the high school. Doctoral dissertation, Duke University, 1965.

2. High School Psychology:
Past Trends and Future Hopes

T. L. ENGLE

Having just completed 49 years of teaching and graduate work, having recently received the title of Professor Emeritus, and having just begun receiving social security checks, I can understand why I was asked to discuss the history of psychology in high schools. For 14 years I taught at the high school level, mostly mathematics but in the later years psychology. Since 1938, I have been teaching at the college level, but I have been active in promoting the teaching of psychology at the high school level.

Today I can wear my convention badge openly, at least around Division 2 (Teaching of Psychology) meetings and hopefully around Division 31 (State Psychological Association) meetings. There was a time when psychologists would see my badge and then verbally attack me for degrading their sacred subject. It was bad enough to attempt to teach psychology to college freshmen or sophomores, but teaching it below college level was treason. I tried to point out that psychology might contain material which would be of value to high school students.

Portions of this chapter have appeared in the *Journal of School Psychology*, Volume 5, 1967.

Also, I would point out that perhaps psychology was not getting its full share of superior students wishing to major in psychology. High school students would be likely to have some idea of chemistry, physics and biology, and decide upon entering college to major in one of those fields, never even considering a mysterious area called psychology. My attackers never seemed to be impressed by my arguments.

As a graduate student in psychology in 1932, taking some work in summer sessions while still teaching in a high school, I thought I could teach psychology in high school more effectively than I could teach mathematics. I spent some time looking over various book exhibits and asked for a high school textbook in psychology. Some salesmen admitted that they had no such book but hastened to add that they had a college textbook which would be just what I needed. The salesman to whom I owe the most asked why I wanted to teach psychology in high school. In fact, I remember his exact words: "Why in Hell do you want to teach that stuff in high school for?" I have spent much of my professional life trying to answer that question.

Finally I did find a 1926 textbook called *Practical Psychology: Human Nature in Everyday Life*. It impressed me as being somewhat of a boiled down college textbook with some of the most interesting parts deleted (Robinson, 1926).

I make no claim to being a true pioneer in the field of high school psychology. In fact, psychology was taught in high schools long before I was born. A two-volume work, *Elements of Mental Philosophy*, first published in 1831, was evidently used in some secondary schools of that decade, but in 1840 it was abridged to a one-volume book for use in academies and high schools (Robach, 1952). In that same year, a teacher in the Geneva Female Seminary published a book based on her lectures, entitled, *Elements of the Philosophy of Mind Applied to the Development of Thought and Feelings* (Louttit, 1956). By 1857 St. Louis offered a high school course in Mental Philosophy which seems to have been somewhat of a psychology course (Coffield and Engle, 1960).

The first high school textbooks containing the word "psychology" in the titles appeared in 1889. In that year, a Professor of Mental and Moral Science at the Michigan State Normal School published a textbook with the impressive title, *Elementary Psychology, or the First Principles of Mental and Moral Science for High, Normal, and other Secondary Schools and for Private Reading.* In the same year, the principal of Wesleyan Academy at Wilbraham, Massachusetts, published *Rudimentary Psychology for Schools and Colleges* which was "designed for students in academies, high schools, and collegiate institutions" (Louttit, 1956). If present-day psychologists wish to save time in writing prefaces for books, they might quote from this author who said, "This is an attempt to present in a clear and easily apprehensible form, with due regard both to scientific requirements and to the consensus of the best and most recent authorities, the main facts of psychology." It has been reported that prior to 1890 there were seven books intended for use in high schools, although in two cases the books were intended for the teacher rather than for the pupils. The number of these 19th-century textbooks underscores a feeling that textbooks for use at the high school level can be counted on the fingers of one hand.

In 1956 an analysis was made of seven textbooks considered by their publishers to have been written for high school courses in psychology. They differed greatly in their treatment of the various areas of psychology. For example, one book devoted one percent of its pages to biological foundations of behavior, another 22 percent to the same topic. The proportions of pages devoted to personality ranged from 15 to 45 percent, learning ranged from 3 to 29 percent, mental hygiene from 11 to 28 percent and social psychology from 0 to 15 percent. Apparently the various authors emphasized what they believed to be important for instruction in psychology at the high school level. No generally recognized guidelines were available (Engle, 1956).

Present day psychologists are not the first to be interested in the teaching of psychology at the secondary level. An examination paper from the Thayer Academy dated 1894 was found in the library of William James. Evidently he did not prepare the examination, but he was interested in the teaching of psychology at the secondary level. One of the questions on the examination was, "Define instinct and illustrate. Show how it may be modified by intelligence" (Roback, 1952).

During the late years of the 19th and early years of the 20th centuries, psychology was offered in high schools in some states, at least in Iowa, as a "professional" course for students who were planning to teach in elementary schools after high school graduation. With this "professional" training in psychology, the high school graduate needed only attend normal school for one semester or summer in order to secure a teacher's license (Engle, 1967b).

Surveys of about 20 years ago indicated that in approximately two-thirds of the high schools offering psychology, it was a one-semester course. It was a two-semester course in the other third. It was principally in the larger school systems that psychology was offered as a separate course of instruction, although sometimes it was offered in surprisingly small high schools (Engle and Bunch, 1956)

(Helfant, 1952). There is some evidence that slightly over half of the students taking psychology in high school planned to enter college and that two-thirds of them were from the upper halves of their high school classes in terms of academic records (Engle, 1958 *a and b*). One survey has indicated that only about 2 percent of the high schools offering psychology do so primarily for students *not* planning to attend college, but that 20 percent offered the course primarily for students planning to attend college. There were a few high schools reporting that they offered two different courses in psychology, one for college-bound students and usually under the title of "Psychology". They offered a different course for students not planning to attend college, usually under a title such as "Human Relationships" (Engle, 1967*a*).

A 1957 survey reported that at that time about 1 student out of 10 taking introductory psychology in 13 universities had had some instruction in psychology in a high school course. Probably the proportion is greater now (Engle, 1957). In the survey, it was reported that of 448 university students having had psychology in high school, 35 percent of those having had a one-semester course and 57 percent of those having had a two-semester course said that their high school courses in psychology had been the primary influence which led them to sign up for an introductory course in psychology in college. Furthermore, when these college students were asked if their high school courses had given them the correct impression of psychology as they had come to know psychology in their university courses, 55 percent replied in the affirmative. In addition, 49 percent expressed the opinion that their high school courses had been of assistance to them in their university courses, while only two percent believed that high school psychology had been a handicap to them. The students who had taken a two-semester course in high school were more likely to believe they had been assisted than did those who had taken only a one-semester course in high school. Remeber that this survey was reported 15 years ago. Have conditions changed?

It is interesting to note that American psychologists are not the only ones concerned about the teaching of psychology at the secondary level. According to a 1969 article in the *Bulletin of the British Psychological Association,* based on a very limited sampling, only about a fourth of the secondary schools in England, Wales, and Scotland taught some form of psychology, girl's schools giving more attention to the subject than boy's or mixed schools. Head teachers gave a clear preference for the human relations rather than the scientific approach, a view which was in marked contrast to that expressed by the heads of departments of psychology in British universities. Even those university professors who favored the introduction of psychology into the British schools were worried about the shortage of suitable people to teach it. Almost all agreed that the psychology taught at teacher-training colleges and by many departments of education in universities was either inadequate or irrelevant to the training of teachers of psychology as such. In conclusion, it was said that the British Society might well express itself by saying that rather than a specific course in psychology, the better course of action would be to introduce something like an interdisciplinary subject under a title such as, "Social and Scientific Foundations of Behaviour." (Westby, 1969)

British school teachers of psychology were reported to be enthusiastic about the potential of psychology as a school subject, although many mentioned difficulties such as their own lack of training, lack of a defined syllabus and lack of suitable textbooks. None expressed worry about the immaturity of their pupils or of a tendency to morbid self-analysis. On the contrary, they reported that pupils found the subject absorbing and no more disturbing than other school subjects. It was concluded that British psychologists should be actively concerned over what is to be taught in the name of psychology, in how it is presented and in the qualifications of those who are to teach it. It was felt that there should be a clear distinction and separation between student counseling and the teaching of psychology.

In the above mentioned article, there is a brief report on the teaching of psychology in the secondary schools of some other countries. For the most part, a traditional philosophical psychology is taught in France. The British journal reported that in Sweden a more academic syllabus is used, with some practical work. The human relations approach is found most wholeheartedly in Australia and Canada. In 1965 I had a letter from an Australian doctoral candidate at the University of Oregon (Kirby, 1965). He felt quite strongly that psychology should be taught at the high school level in his country because, as he said, "the philosophies and methods of secondary schools lend themselves to a thorough and deep coverage of curriculum subjects." He planned to commence a modest campaign to have psychology added to the curriculum of New South Wales high schools, and at the time, he was preparing an article for the *New South Wales Educational Gazette*. At the 1972 meetings of the International Congress of Psychology in Tokyo, I talked with one psychologist from Australia, who said that psychology is not taught below the college level in his country.

Reporting on the United States, the above mentioned British journal stated that there is a great variation from state to state, a statement with which American psychologists agree. Also, it was said that in the United States there tends to be a rather superficial human relations approach, although a more rigorous discipline is attempted in some places.

Recently I have been corresponding with a doctoral candidate in West Germany (Lehmeier, 1972). He is working on a thesis concerned with the teaching of psychology at the high school level. He reports that in Germany psychology has just been introduced as a school subject in some classes of the last grades of high school, and that his thesis on this topic is the first as far as he has been able to learn.

At the 1972 meetings of the International Congress of Psychology I contacted ten Japanese psychologists and asked them whether psychology is taught below the college level in Japan. Apparently psychology is not offered as a separate course in the secondary schools of Japan, but some material of a psychological nature is presented as units in such courses as ethics and social studies. The psychologists said they hoped to give a more favorable report by the time of the 1976 meetings in Paris.

One of my hopes is that someone will make an international study of the teaching of psychology at the pre-college level.

What kind of teachers teach psychology at the high school level? The surveys have shown that these teachers tend to have slightly over five years of college training and tend to be teachers with five or more years of teaching experience. A few of them devote full time to the teaching of psychology but most of them teach in one or more other areas, especially social studies. However, a considerable number teach science, mathematics, or do administrative or guidance work. If we consider their training in departments of psychology plus their training in educational psychology, they have a mean number of 12 undergraduate and about 6½ hours of graduate training. However, if one considers training in departments of psychology only, the figure drops to a little less than 6 hours undergraduate plus 2½ hours graduate training (Engle, 1952a). A recent study in western New York State tends to verify this statement, the mode for that study being 8 hours (Abrams & Stanley, 1967).

The APA Education and Training Board Committee on Psychology in Secondary Schools is concerned about this problem of training. In a report prepared by this committee (Abrams & Stanley, 1967) it is indicated that only 50 percent of the states certify teaching majors in psychology. In the other states students wishing to prepare for teaching psychology must usually have two majors, one being in an area which can be certified. Also, this committee has reported that fewer than one college in 100 offers a methods course in the teaching of psychology, and that fewer than one of three colleges offering a teaching major or minor provide for student practice teaching in psychology. Three sentences from this committee's report are of special interest: "There is an abundant supply of students who want to be prepared and of institutions that want to prepare them, but this is generally as far as it goes.... There is a long way to go before high-quality high school teachers of psychology will be turned out in large quantities. 'Retreading' of already certified teachers during summer sessions may be needed to augment the baccalaureate-level trickle until it becomes more of a torrent."

What are most high school courses in psychology like? Essentially, we do not know. We do have some reports of questionnaire surveys, but there is always the question as to what kind of persons respond to questionnaires and with what accuracy (Engle, 1957).

We have evidence that high school textbooks devote less space to biological foundations of behavior, learning and statistics than do introductory college textbooks. On the other hand, the high school textbooks tend to devote more space to personality, personal problems, and mental health than do college textbooks (Engle, 1956).

For supplemental reading, teachers tend to assign "psychological" articles in such popular magazines as *Readers Digest, Saturday Evening Post,* and *Life,* largely because there are no APA or other authentic psychological journals suitable for use at the high school level (Engle, 1955).

We have evidence that most high schools consider psychology as part of the Social Studies curriculum rather than as part of the Sciences curriculum (Engle, 1951 & 1952b).

When teachers have been asked to rank objectives for their courses in psychology, they tended to place at the top of their lists the objective of assisting students in solving their personal problems. When asked to rank subject matter areas in the order of emphasis in their courses, teachers tended to place material on mental health and individuality at the top of their lists. They placed statistics at the bottom of their lists. However, it should be added that about one-third of the teachers gave as their primary objective the development of an appreciation for psychology as a field of scientific knowledge, including a fundamental technical vocabulary and familiarity with basic research methods. These teachers, when asked to rank the subject matter areas in the order of emphasis in their courses, placed learning at the top of the list, with mental health material running a rather close second place. These scientifically oriented teachers did place somewhat more emphasis on sensation and perception, and statistics, than did teachers whose primary objective was that of assisting students with solutions to personal problems (Engle, 1967a).

Having surveyed the past and present of high school psychology, attention must be given to the possible future, although prophesying is always a dangerous business. In 1966 each member of the Committee on High School Psychology, APA Division on the Teaching of Psychology, and each member of the APA Education and Training Board Committee on Psychology in Secondary Schools was asked for his opinion as to what is likely to happen in the field of high school psychology. It was suggested that replies might be made in terms of what they would like to see happen in the future (Engle, 1967b).

One of the questions asked was "Do you think psychology will continue to be offered in the senior, or junior and senior, years; or will it come to be offered at the freshman or sophomore levels?" The psychologists who replied were agreed that a course in psychology should continue to be offered at the senior, or junior and senior, level of the high school. Some qualified their answers, for example: "While I believe certain psychological materials should be infused with other freshman and sophomore courses, I'm against a separate course at these levels," and "I think psychology in high schools should be offered to seniors only, unless it is some hygiene or family living course disguised as psychology."

Another question asked was, "Do you think the present emphasis on mental health will continue or will psychology come to be generally recognized as a high school science?" Respondents wrote at considerable length in answering this question. One psychologist said, "Might it not be well to face this dual system squarely and propose two different types of psychology courses: one emphasizing mental hygiene, dating, and so on, and the other being essentially a standard college course in psychology offered in the senior year of high school to exceptionally able, well-prepared, college-bound students? To try to meet the needs of both groups in the same classrooms seems doomed to failure." Another psychologist said, "Obviously there are two jobs to be done in which the profession of psychology must play an important role. One of these is the mental health, happy family-life problem. This type of thing is not the sole prerogative of our profession, so why label it 'psychology?' We are only one of several profession-sciences which offer significant contributions to this important social problem. The other job is to teach high school pupils something about psychology as a science of behavior, and here our responsibility is even greater." A slightly different point of view was expressed by one psychologist who said, "It is my belief that we must have two approaches, the mental hygiene and the scientific. Those students who do not go to college may find this the only formal training they will ever receive in mental hygiene. I would not like to see psychology at the high school level taught entirely as a science. I think we are limiting our influence if we take this position." Another said, "High school psychology has gotten more over into the scientific method. This I am glad of, but don't ever expect that the adjustment aspect will or should be left out of general psychology, not even at the college level." One psychologist who has conducted summer institutes for high school teachers of psychology said, "Many teachers state that their students want to do independent projects, often for Science Fairs, dealing with animal behavior, but they do not feel competent to supervise such projects. In a few cases I have had applications from science supervisors or supporting letters from principals implying dissatisfaction with the mental health approach and indicating a sincere interest in developing a scientific approach to the study of behavior. I believe there is a growing interest in high school psychology as a science and many high school teachers of psychology recognize the inadequacy of their training in statistics and experimental methodology. They are eager to improve their background in these areas. Timid administrators will gradually drop those courses which are designed primarily to provide group therapy. Some principals have been embarrassed by over zealous teachers of such courses." A slightly different point of view was expressed by one psychologist who said, "Present pressures for more and more college level work taught in the high schools should work in favor of an elective course in scientific psychology in the better academic high schools. On the other hand, an increasingly larger percentage of the total age group persists through the eleventh and twelfth grades, thereby creating the need for simplified courses such as the mental hygiene approach to psychology." A final quotation brings the American Psychological Association directly into the picture. "If APA can exert some leadership in having an advanced placement course in scientific psychology prepared so that the exceptionally able student can take the Advanced Placement Examination of the College Entrance Examination Board and receive credit or waivers in college, I believe that the present mental hygiene emphasis can be counteracted somewhat with a more scientific one."

A third question was: "What is likely to happen, should happen, in the way of preparation requirements for teachers of psychology?" It is generally assumed that most teachers of high school psychology are inadequately prepared and, as has been indicated, there is some statistical justification for this assumption. But one psychologist said, "I did a survey three years ago on qualifications of a small sampling of high school teachers and others have done the same. I was surprised to find that teachers had more hours of courses in psychology than we had expected. People tend to generalize from special cases where the high school psychology teacher has almost no background for the subject." One university professor said, "About half of our students are in teacher preparation areas, some who want to teach psychology. With a minimum of twenty-seven hours for a major or twenty-one semester hours for a minor, they will be better qualified than the average person presently teaching high school psychology. I have to admit that I 'indoctrinate' them toward high school psychology." The general trend of the responses seems to be that, for the present, summer institutes are the best answer to the upgrading of high school teachers of psychology. As one psychologist said, "I would like to see a considerable number of major universities offer, during summers, a systematic program leading to a master's degree in the teaching of high school psychology for persons already certified to be high school teachers."

Another of the questions asked was "Is the number of high schools offering psychology likely to increase?" In general the respondents tended to reply in the affirmative, but with some reservations. One psychologist suggested that there are four factors tending to slow down the increment: (1) due to reorganization and consolidation there are fewer high schools that can offer psychology; (2) the already crowded curriculum cannot take on another 'college' subject; (3) there is a lack of adequately trained teachers; (4) because of the present-day emphasis on 'science', psychology cannot be offered. (It is assumed that most readers of this article will disagree with the implication that psychology is not a science.) "It seems to me that it is questionable whether some of the very small schools should offer the course because they are not likely to have qualified teachers." One psychologist who has conducted summer institutes for high school teachers of psychology believes that there is a gradual increase in the number of high schools offering psychology as an elective and that there is a growing interest on the part of biology and general science teachers in the science of behavior. Another psychologist pointed out that there is an ever increasing number of journal articles concerning high school psychology, that summer institutes for high school teachers are meeting with marked success, and today many Science Fair exhibits are concerned with psychological topics, such as animal learning, even though they might not be classified as psychology. A final response to be quoted is, "I think there will be very little immediate change unless there is some definite leadership from APA at large, from some committee of APA, or best of all, from state psychological associations."

This quotation leads us to the last question, "If psychology continues to be taught in high schools what leadership is likely to be offered by APA?" It must be remembered that the following comments were made by psychologists who are interested enough in high school psychology to serve on APA committees concerned with this problem. The comments may not be representative of APA as a whole. One psychologist said, "The emphasis is on need. If APA offers help, we can begin to upgrade the teachers, the course, and the level of efficiency of students. Until this happens there is going to be very little change because teachers are generally caught up in too many other things. APA needs to carry the big stick with an even bigger voice." Another said, "I have no idea what

APA is likely to do. My hope is that we will provide or obtain the financial support necessary for the development of suitable curricular materials for high school courses. Perhaps APA could obtain foundation support for course material projects." To quote another psychologist, "I'm afraid that APA will not in the immediate future lead the way. We still have a large number of psychologists who believe that psychology should not be taught in high schools. But we are teaching psychology at the high school level right now and regardless of whether or not we think it advisable, we are faced with the problem of having unqualified teachers teaching psychology. In other words, it is here now and we should do our best to do everything we can to help out. Along with trying to get better teachers we should help to raise certification requirements and try to get more states, eventually all of them, to certify psychology at the high school level. I do know that a large number of high school teachers of psychology are looking for help and wanting it, as evidenced by the fact that I answer a dozen or more letters every week from such individuals who are seeking help. They want it, need it, and will use it, if we can make information and news available to them." Perhaps the attitude of the psychologists is well summed up in the statement of one who said, "APA should not reduce its involvement in this area, but we may need to think of more effective ways of providing positive influence."

I have been asked, on the basis of my rather long past experience, to predict what may or should be the future of the teaching of psychological material in secondary schools. I shall conclude with a few crystal-ball thoughts or hopes, risky as this may be.

1. Over the years, I have received many letters from teachers asking for help. I did what I could through

correspondence and teacher's manuals. It is gratifying to know that now APA has an office devoted to pre-college psychology and publishes a paper, *Periodically,* and other material.

2. It is also gratifying to note that APA now has a proposed high school curriculum development project. At long last, some guide lines for authors may be available.

3. Valuable as the APA Washington office is to teachers, there is need for more intimate communication between psychologists and high school teachers. I hope that I can predict that state associations, and local associations, will invite teachers to become affiliated with them, or at least invite them to attend some of their meetings.

4. I hope that psychologists in the various states will make themselves available to speak to high school classes, and to help students with such problems as come up in connection with Science Fair projects.

5. Although many high school teachers have had very limited training in psychology, there are some who have had excellent training. Within the various states I hope that something can be done so the college freshmen with a good background in high school psychology will not have to take the introductory college course in psychology. High schools usually operate on five class meetings a week rather than the three traditional meetings for college classes. With more time and under well-trained and enthusiastic teachers, why should college students repeat their introduction to psychology, possibly under a graduate student whose interests may be in fields other than teaching? Also, remember that some high schools devote two semesters to psychology.

6. In the past, and at present, high school courses have often stressed mental hygiene and a human relations approach bordering on how to win friends and influence people. This human relations approach has often stressed problems of romantic love, a topic which may now be more suitable for junior-high and even elementary school pupils. Isn't it time to turn away form the emphasis on teaching students how, by one means or another, they can manage to live with other people? Shouldn't we teach them about how psychologists are able to study social problems, especially in small-group research where many variables can be controlled? There are many opportunities here for high school students to do some "research" of their own.

7. Maybe as I gaze into the crystal ball I see a lessening of emphasis on the teaching of psychology as a course in high school, but an increasing of emphasis on development of modules concerned with psychological material and incorporated into curriculum units devoted to behavioral sciences.

8. We seem to be entering a period when the teaching of psychology at the secondary school level is being introduced and developed in a number of countries other than the United States. May we hope that the international interest of adolescents in the science of behavior will serve as one step toward better world social conditions?

REFERENCES

Abrams, A. M. & Stanley, J. C. Preparation of high school psychology teachers by colleges. *American Psychologist* 1967, 22, 166-169.

American Psychological Association, Committee to Study Problems Connected with the Teaching of Psychology. Report A. Survey on teaching psychology in secondary schools. *Psychological Bulletin,* 1937, **34,** 660-674.

Coffield, K. E., & Engle, T. L. High school psychology; A history and some observations, *American Psychologist,* 1960, **15,** 350-352.

Engle, T. L. A national survey of the teaching of psychology in high schools, *School Review,* 1951, **59,** 467-471.

Engle, T. L. The training and experience of high school teachers of psychology. *Educational Administration, & Supervision,* 1952, **38,** 91-96.

Engle, T. L. Teaching of psychology in high schools, *American Psychologist,* 1952, **7,** 31-35.

Engle, T. L. Methods and techniques used in teaching psychology in high schools, *Social Education,* 1955, **19,** 346-348.

Engle, T. L. High school psychology, *Contemporary Psychology,* 1956, **1,** 140-143.

Engle, T. L. High school psychology courses as related to university psychology courses, *Bulletin of the National Association of Secondary School Principals,* 1957, **41,** 38-42.

Engle, T. L. College plans and scholastic standing of students taking psychology in high school, *Bulletin of the National Association of Secondary Schools Prinicipals,* 1958, **42,** 92-93.

Engle T. L. University psychology students having had psychology in high school. *American Psychologist,* 1958, **13,** 116-117.

Engle, T. L. Objectives for and subject matter stressed in high school courses in psychology, *American Psychologist,* 1967, **22,** 162-166.

Engle, T. L. Teaching psychology at the secondary school

level: Past, present, possible future. *Journal of School Psychology,* 1967, 5, 168-176.

Engle, T. L., & Bunch, M. E. The teaching of psychology in high school, *American Psychologist,* 1956, 11, 188-193.

Goodale, R. A. A survey of high school teachers of psychology in Massachusetts. *Teaching of Psychology Newsletter,* June, 1970, 7-8.

Helfant, K. The teaching of psychology in high schools: A review of the literature. *School Review,* 1952, 60, 467-473.

Hunt, R. G., Bodin, A. M., Patti, J., & Rookey, E. Psychology in the secondary school curricula of western New York. *Teaching of Psychology Newsletter,* June, 1969, 4-6.

Johnson, J. M. An experimental design for a General Psychology course, *Social Sciences,* 1970, 3, 35-43.

Kirby, R. J., Department of Psychology, University of Oregon, Eugene, Oregon 97403. (Letter dated May 12, 1965)

Lehmeier, H., Dipl.-Psych., 6056 Heusenstamm, Odenwaldstr. 16, West Germany. (Letters dated April 16, 1972 and July 15, 1972)

Louttit, C. M. Psychology in nineteenth century high schools. *American Psychologist,* 1956, 11, 717.

Perkins, H. J. Research: Key to learning and teaching. *Commission on Undergraduate Education in the Biological Sciences,* 1969, 5, 1-3.

Roback, A. A. Psychology in American secondary schools in the 90's. *American Psychologist,* 1952, 7, 44-45.

Robinson, E. S. *Practical psychology: Human nature in everday life.* New York: Macmillan, 1926.

Schumacher, G. Survey of psychology in Ohio high schools. *Periodically,* 1972, 2, 1.

University of the State of New York, The State Education

Department, Bureau of Secondary Curriculum Development. *Social Studies Curriculum,* Albany, New York, 1967.

University of the State of New York, The State Education Department. Bureau of Seconday Curriculum Development. *A New Style of Certification,* Albany, New York, 1971.

Westby, G. Report of the working party on the teaching of psychology in schools. *Bulletin of the British Psychological Society,* 1969, **22,** 103-108.

3. High School Psychology Courses: To Be or Not to Be?

RICHARD A. KASSCHAU

> To be, or not to be, that is the question:
> Whether 'tis nobler in the mind to suffer
> the slings and arrows of outrageous fortune,
> Or to take arms against a sea of troubles
> And by opposing end them. To die: to sleep.
> No more; and by a sleep to say we end
> The heart-ache and the thousand natural shocks
> That flesh is heir to: 'tis a consummation
> Devoutly to be wish'd. To die: to sleep.
> To sleep? perchance to dream. Ay, there's the rub;
> For in that sleep of death what dreams may come,
> When we have shuffled off this mortal coil,
> Must give us pause. . .
>   — Shakespeare

I would like to ask you to pause with me at this point to consider psychology's "sea of troubles" in the area of pre-college curriculum development, to consider the curriculum development dreams turned nightmare of other disciplines, and to draw from those dreams some lessons for psychology. The data are quite clearcut — I hope the lessons can be cleanly drawn.

As you drift down through the four stages of sleep (Kleitman, 1963), so as to reach Emergent Stage I in which dreaming occurs, let me see if I can accelerate your descent

45

by reviewing some of the statistics concerning high school psychology — statistics which very clearly delineate some of our troubles. Those who have been following the enrollment figures in the various high school subject areas will be familiar with trends such as those reported by Schumacher (1971). He reports that in the interval from 1966 to 1971 the number of psychology courses offered in Ohio jumped from 50 to 345, and the number of schools in which psychology was offered rose from 45 to 292. Accompanying this change was a jump in the number of psychology teachers from 50 to 326, and in the number of students enrolled in psychology from 3,400 to 17,600. That means in terms of the customer (i.e., the student), interest in psychology has been growing at the rate of 40 percent a year in Ohio for 5 years. Similarly, in South Carolina, in 1966 10,400 students were enrolled in psychology courses whereas in the 1971 academic year 15,700 students were enrolled in psychology. Thus, in South Carolina enrollment has been growing at the rate of 8 percent per year. The trends vary, but they consistently show substantial growth as has also been reported in California (Parrott and Setz, 1970) and Maine (Chapko and Fuchs, 1972).

However, this fantastic increase in enrollment has, as noted by Schumacher (1971), created a very serious problem. The five- to sevenfold increase in student enrollees has not been accompanied by a similar increase in the rate of training high school psychology teachers. The necessary result is that more and more inadequately prepared teachers are going to be asked, or volunteer, to teach psychology to high school students. Data gathered by the American Psychological Association in the summer of 1970 indicated that at that time the average teacher of high school psychology had had somewhere between 8 and

13 undergraduate hours of psychology. Ryan (1972), sampling teachers who applied for a summer training institute, reported somewhat more encouraging figures regarding teacher preparation. The median number of courses previously taken by such teachers was listed to be eight. However, it should be remembered this was a sample of teachers sufficiently motivated to apply for a summer institute so as to improve their own training. Nonetheless, the problem remains.

One result of increased enrollment and more teachers has been a steadily increasing number of requests to the American Psychological Association from high school psychology teachers. These requests take various forms but essentially boil down to one phrase: "Help me!" In a broader sense, and seemingly in response to these pleas, a number of new magazines specifically intended for high school psychology teachers have been inaugurated in the last two years. These include the refreshing *People-Watching* which focuses on a broad variety of intellectual and pragmatic issues concerning precollege psychology, the news and information oriented *Periodically,* and the about-to-be-published *Behavioral and Social Science Teacher.* Yet problems remain: the May, 1972 issue of the *American Psychologist* addressed a special topic — "Psychology's Manpower: The Education and Utilization of Psychologists" — but the entire issue was addressed to graduate education. For example, one article entitled "Getting your first job: A view from the bottom" was written by the holder of a doctorate! High school psychology, from both the teacher's and student's perspective, was almost completely ignored in the issue.

The problems are several. Let's look first of all at the high school student likely to want to take psychology, second at some of the curriculum development efforts of other disciplines and finally at how the changing student and prior curriculum efforts might be focused on what psychology ought to do.

James Morris, as Commissioner of Higher Education for South Carolina has noted (1971) that of all the students entering the educational system at the first grade in South Carolina only 50 percent will stay to graduate from some high school. Of that group only about 33 percent will go on to some form of higher education, and of that group something less than 50 percent (or 8 percent of the beginning total) will enroll in some form of college or university education. Yet with improved educational techniques, the greater emphasis being placed on the importance of a high school diploma, and the many changes being wrought by desegregation, these percentages are constantly shifting.

Two points need to be made. First, it seems to be obvious folly to address a discipline-based high school curriculum to only 8 percent of the total school population. Second, and more importantly, one of the major effects of these processes is to introduce into the system of public education what Klingelhofer (1972) has labeled "the new student". In the past these students have been labeled "disadvantaged", "high-risk", or "culturally different" but they are typified by Blacks, Indians, Puerto Ricans, Mexican-Americans, etc. Klingelhofer goes on to note that the universe of new students is considerably broader and more complex that has previously been recognized. He notes that the curricular strategies which respond effectively to the particular qualities of these various subgroups of new students must be examined closely. But my primary point in mentioning Klingelhofer is to point to his conclusion that as conventionally taught, the introductory psychology course is both highly verbal and conceptual, both abstract and traditional — exactly the attributes which have been turning students away in record numbers from enrolling in physics and chemistry. It must be noted that without help from academic and professional psychologists, these "poorly prepared" teachers of high school psychology have managed to quintuple student enrollment in high school psychology in five years. If academic, discipline-oriented psychologists hope to "teach psychology correctly" we should at least take the precaution of looking at other successful and unsuccessful curriculum development projects, find out why students are currently enrolling in psychology, and involve these (highly successful) high school teachers of psychology in our efforts.

In a report concerning career decisions of talented youths (Watley & Nichols, 1969), it is noted that the percentage of male National Merit finalists who chose physics as a college major dropped from 18.8 to 11.2 during the sixties; while the percentage of those choosing to go into engineering fell from 29.6 to 17.6 during the same interval. Professor Laurel Tanner (1972) in addressing this shift has suggested that a lack of social relevance in the science curriculum is at the heart of the problem. In analyzing the types of curriculum packages developed by the basic disciplines (with substantial, multimillion dollar support from NSF) she notes that the curricula which were produced represent (1) an over emphasis of basic science at the expense of applied science, (2) a mode of thinking which does not allow for humane reflections or interpretations and (3) the valuing of research over action. In essence, each discipline, with substantial input from the college-level academician, seems to have produced a minature replica of itself with the effect of creating what Tanner calls a laminated curriculum — a layer of chemistry, a layer of physics. . . . The essence of Tanner's recommended solution to counteract the swing away from science is exemplified by a comment from the British Council for Scientific Policy which concluded in addressing the same declining interest in science in Britain that "science must be presented in a unified and unfragmented way as an exciting activity in human life and society."

So the time is at hand to consider how best to formalize a psychology curriculum for use in high schools. We have a rapidly expanding base of interested students, a large cadre of ill-prepared teachers, and numerous precedents established by our sister disciplines (sociology and biology) concerning the implementation of curriculum development efforts. Let me simply list seven goals that I think a national psychology curriculum development project should achieve.

First, *define the target population*. Because psychology is already the most popular undergraduate major at the college level, and because of figures such as those cited by Commissioner Morris regarding the relatively small proportion of the total population which is admitted to college, the high school psychology curriculum should be aimed at non-college-bound students. Given the verbal, abstract nature of the typical college introductory psychology course, it should be possible to develop a high school course which emphasizes the pragmatic, the applied, in such a way as not to hinder college-bound students who also take psychology in the high school. Indeed, such a course could provide a very firm base for subsequent college-level courses, although I do not think this should be a major goal.

Second, *start "where the kids are at"*. If you read a high school manual or college catalog particularly looking for the expressed goals of these institutions, you see phrases like "advancement of knowledge," "freedom of inquiry" and "creative production". Yet, if you talk to students in these institutions concerning why they are there, you hear phrases such as "required," "dates" and "get a job". For too long the disparity between these goals or reasons has been neglected. It is incumbent upon the prime movers that if a nationally coordinated curriculum development project is to be started, they must look first at student goals and expectations concerning psychology in the high schools.

Third, *use the principles of the discipline in teaching the discipline*. Psychology is perhaps unique in having within its sphere of interest the principles which can be most effectively used in presenting the discipline. Yet, one need only pick up the typical introductory psychology text to find evidence of the extent to which such principles as distribution of practice, reinforcement and those concerning how to get and hold attention have been ignored. Effective utilization of the principles of learning could have the double benefit not only of (1) increasing student retention of relevant materials, but also of (2) increasing teacher effectiveness over the long run.

Fourth, *involve high school teachers and students*. The SRSS curriculum project of the American Sociological Association went a long way toward involving most of the relevant parties in the development of their high school curriculum packages. However, they were as guilty as most projects of ignoring the ultimate consumer — the high school student. While few curriculum development projects have completed their work without benefit of formative evaluation by high school students, assurance that the project is addressed specifically to the target population can be greatly increased by involving students in the initial phases of developing the materials.

Fifth, assure *flexibility*. Once developed, psychology must fit into a high school schedule already crowded with four years of English, one to several years of required social studies, and numerous other disciplines competing for attention during the remaining eight to eleven credits. The teachers, in turn, must face five or six classes a day five days a week. Students, and especially as mentioned earlier "the new students", come from increasingly diverse racial, ethnic, and economic backgrounds. So what is needed is a course with flexibility for high school administrators faced with tight schedules and shifting demands, teachers of varied backgrounds and busy schedules who face the prospect of teaching the same material up to six times a day, and an increasingly diverse group of students.

Sixth, the content of the course should stress, insofar as possible, an *interdisciplinary* approach to psychology. The course needs to be interdisciplinary in the sense of expanding the content of psychology so as to show the interface between psychology and its sister sciences of sociology and biology. However, this interdisciplinary aspect can be assured by more basic means. For example, a primary teaching goal of the project as a whole must be to indicate what men have in common as individuals and as members of society. This is a goal which should pervade all aspects of the final product of the project.

Seventh, the project must have *relevance*. I refer here to the empirical definition of relevance as the term is used by students and defined by Menges and Trumpeter (1972). Relevance involves elements of utility, difficulty, dynamism, and interest. Having read their article, you might think this is a broad order, but as a general goal for psychology's curriculum efforts it is not an effort to be ignored.

Such an effort is not to be taken lightly nor has the American Psychological Association initiated its curriculum development project without considerable thought. Most recently, Barry Markman of Wayne State University and myself have had a project which has been funded by USOE and viewed as a prototypic effort for the larger scale effort now being initiated. Let me paint for you a brief picture of our project as it has evolved. What Markman and I have proposed is that the final psychology curriculum package be composed of a number of individual units, where each self-contained unit would constitute an average of two weeks of teaching materials. The units as a whole, would be expected to more than adequately represent all of the subject matter of psychology, ranging from the most abstract experimental topics to the most pragmatic issues surrounding sex, love, dating, marriage, drugs, etc. Flexibility is already introduced in terms of allowing the teacher complete freedom over the order in which these units would be presented, and indeed, which units would even be presented.

To get a better feeling for a specific unit let me simply describe the unit on "Black/White America" which was developed at the University of South Carolina this past summer and is currently being pilot-tested. The unit is composed of 37 separate one-day activities — much more material than could possibly be taught in the two-week interval for which the unit is designed. On some days the teacher is given no choice; there is a single exercise which the developing group of two high school psychology teachers, two high school students and I viewed to be of sufficient importance and interest that it should be taught as an integral part of the unit. On other days, the teacher is offered as many as eight options in choosing which specific activity to offer. This combination of required and optional exercises offers the teacher some 109,000 different ways of presenting the two week unit! The single one-hour exercises are provided in sufficient variety so that the teacher can teach an all-white, a mixed black-and-white, or an all-black classroom. In addition, the unit provides sufficient hints so that the teacher would be able, when faced with a unisex classroom or one with a prepondance of Puerto Ricans, Mexicans or other minority group, to revise the unit so as to make sex rather than race the basis for definition of a minority to be studied. The unit as a whole involves games, role playing, definitions, and in general, a broad variety of activities both individual and group. Not surprisingly, the initial pilot test results indicate a direct correlation between student interest and the extent to which student responses and experiences could positively influence in-class content.

In summary, our proposal would be that the curriculum development project be constituted of a number of teaching packages covering from perhaps one or two days to several weeks of information. There should be more of these packages than could be offered in two semesters. The various packages should (1) represent a broad interdisciplinary approach to psychology, (2) offer the teacher a variety of means by which to teach the unit, (3) offer the students numerous means for influencing course content both in terms of their own interest and their prior experience and finally (4) offer the teacher a variety of possibilities in terms of both content and technique.

The lessons from other disciplines are clear, the time to act is now, and the task remaining is gigantic; that is, the preparation of a scientifically acceptable curriculum for the presentation of psychology in the high school to a diverse and expanding group of latently interested students. With some help from history and some goals to aim toward, by addressing our discipline and the curriculum development project to the appropriate students, and by involving teachers, students and psychologists in the task, the job can be done. If we take arms against our sea of troubles now, we can, by opposing, end them.

REFERENCES

Chapko, M. K., & Fuchs, A. F. The teaching of psychology in Maine High Schools. Unpublished manuscript, Bowdoin College, 1972.

Kleitman, N. *Sleep and wakefulness,* (Rev. ed.) Chicago: University of Chicago Press, 1963.

Klingelhofei, E. L. Psychology and the new student. *Teaching of Psychology Newsletter,* March 1972, 1.

Menges, R. J., & Trumpeter, P. W. Toward an empirical definition of relevance in undergraduate instruction. *American Psychologist,* 1972, 27, 213-217.

Morris, J. A. Public education and psychology in South Carolina. Colloquium presented at University of South Carolina November 18, 1971.

Parrott, G. L., & Setz, G. Psychology in California high schools. *Teaching of Psychology Newsletter,* December 1970, 10-11.

Ryan, J. J. A survey of high school psychology teachers and course characteristics. *Teaching of Psychology Newsletter,* June 1972, 6.

Schumacher, G. M. High school psychology in Ohio, 1966-1971. *Ohio Psychologist,* 1971, 18, 5-6.

Tanner, L. N. The swing away from science. *Educational Forum,* 1972, 36, 229-238.

Watley, D.J., & Nichols, R. C. *Career decisions of talented youth: Trends over the past decade.* Evanston, Illinois: National Merit scholarship Corporation, 1969.

4. A Survey of High School Psychology: Teacher and Course Characteristics

JAMES J. RYAN

There are a number of recent indications that psychology is being offered as a separate subject in high school with increasing frequency (Gnagey, 1971; Parrott and Setz, 1970; Thornton and Williams, 1971).[1] Because of the low frequency with which it has been taught in the past, it is not likely that many secondary teachers have obtained an educational background specifically intended for teaching psychology courses. Also there appear to be few teacher-training institutions explicitly concerned with preparing teachers in this area or in the behavioral sciences generally. However, with an increased interest in offering psychology at the pre-college level, it will become necessary to plan appropriate educational programs and curricula to ensure the availability of teachers adequately prepared to teach in this and possibly related behavioral science subjects.

As a basis for planning either regular educational curricula or special programs such as summer institutes, workshops, etc., for those who might teach psychology at the secondary level, data were systematically gathered from several sources to obtain some necessary information

[1] Among these is the establishment (May, 1970) of the APA Clearinghouse on Precollege Psychology and its publication *Periodically*.

relevant to these educational decisions. The information obtained concerned mainly the educational background and teaching responsibilities of those presently teaching high school psychology and the instructional content and nature of such courses. Information was obtained from two sources: (1) a questionnaire distributed to psychology teachers in high schools in four adjacent upper Midwest states — Wisconsin, Minnesota, Illinois, and Iowa and (2) application forms submitted by applicants to a National Science Foundation sponsored summer institute for psychology teachers at the secondary level.

SAMPLES

Upper Midwest Questionnaire (UMQ) Sample

A questionnaire was sent to a total of 429 individual schools or teachers in four states: Wisconsin, Iowa, Minnesota and Illinois. In two of the states, Wisconsin and Illinois, questionnaires were sent initially to all teachers included on listings of those teaching psychology provided by the respective State Department of Public Instruction. In the other two states similar lists were not obtained and the questionnaires were addressed directly to "Psychology Teacher" and sent to each public high school in the state having graduating classes of 200 or more pupils as reported for the most recent year (1968-1969) in the USOE Directory of Public Secondary Schools.[2] In addition to the questionnaires, respondents were asked to provide names

[2]*Directory of Public and Secondary Day Schools, 1968-69: Vol. II Great Lakes and Plains Region.* National Center for Educational Statistics. Office of Education, Department of Health, Education, and Welfare.

of any other psychology teachers in their school system. Additional questionnaires were sent to the names so provided if they were not already recipients. This questionnaire was distributed during the 1970-1971 school year.

Table 1 shows the numbers sent and returned in each state and the proportions included in the final samples used for analysis. Of the total 145, 139 returns were from persons presently teaching at least one course in psychology. Since the concern was mainly with those actually teaching psychology, the remaining tabulations and analyses were made only for the latter 139 respondents.

SIA Sample

The summer institute applicant (SIA) sample consisted of those who submitted completed application forms to attend one (at the University of Wisconsin - La Crosse) of the two summer institutes in psychology[3] funded by the National Science Foundation for the summer of 1971. Brochures describing the general nature and objectives of the UW-L institute were distributed directly to the majority of relatively larger high schools in about 12 central and upper midwest states. In addition, the NSF

Table 1
Upper Midwest Questionnaire Sample

	Wisconsin	Minnesota	Iowa	Illinois	Total
Number Sent	112	93	45	179	429
Number Returned	42	31	20	52	145
Number Used	40	28	19	52	139
Percent Used of Number Sent	35	30	42	29	31

[3] The other institute was conducted at State University College, Potsdam, New York.

circulates to all secondary schools in the United States listings of and application procedures for all summer institutes in science and mathematics which included the UW-L institute.

The institute conducted by the UW-L Psychology Department was entitled "Topics and Methods in Experimental Psychology" and was indicated as being for psychology teachers. The other (Potsdam) institute was entitled "Principles of Animal Behavior" and was intended for teachers of natural sciences as well as psychology. Since it appears that the content and objectives of the UW-L institute were closer to the subject matter concerns of the typical high school psychology teacher than were those of the other institute, it does not seem likely that the availability of the alternate institute may have in itself substantially affected the characteristics of the UW-L applicant sample. Nonetheless, independent of the other institute, the content as well as other characteristics of the UW-L institute, e.g., its geographic location, accommodations, level of compensation, length, etc., no doubt did have some selective affects on the characteristics of the applicant sample. The SIA sample, however, does serve as a separate sample of high school psychology teachers which can provide some information concerning their background and characteristics and some indication of the generality of the information obtained in the UMQ sample.

Of the 135 completed applications 26 were from individuals that, at the time, (1970-1971) were not teaching psychology and consequently were not included in the sample for which results will be reported. The total N for this sample was then 109.

QUESTIONNAIRES

The upper midwest sample questionnaire (UMQ) was prepared to obtain information concerning the teachers' formal educational background, present professional and teaching responsibilities and certain characteristics of the psychology course being taught.

The summer institute applicant information was obtained from standard forms prepared by the NSF to be used for this purpose. Certain items were modified slightly to be more appropriate for the subject matter emphasis (psychology) of the institute for which they were used.

A number of the items in the questionnaire and the application forms were essentially identical permitting the results to be summarized in the same form and comparisons to be made between the two samples.

RESULTS

Professional Responsibilities

Respondents in both samples were asked to indicate what positions they filled in their school. The results are shown in Table 2.

Table 2
Principle Position Held

Sample	Teacher	Counselor	Administrator	Teacher & Counselor	Teacher & Administrator
UMQ *N*	120	6	1	10	2
percentage	86	4	1	7	1
SIA *N*	105	3	0	0	1
percentage	96	3	0	0	1

In the UMQ sample, of the 19 respondents who indicated they had professional responsibilities other than teaching, 68 percent also indicated that psychology was the only subject they taught. (In contrast, psychology was the only subject taught by 28 percent of the remaining sample engaged exclusively in teaching.) The smaller proportion of those in the SIA sample having nonteaching responsibilities than in the UMQ sample may have resulted from the requirement that institute participants who held nonteaching positions (e.g., counselors, etc.) must be teaching at least two psychology classes. Another selective factor in the SIA sample was that those with 12-month administrative positions would be less likely to apply for a summer institute even though they were teaching two courses in psychology.

It is quite evident that the greatest proportion of high school psychology courses are taught by full-time teachers rather than on a part-time basis by those who are mainly engaged in providing psychological services in the school setting. This is not to say, however, that a certain proportion of those teaching full time have not had graduate training in counseling and guidance as shown below. It is of interest to note also that there were no school psychologists in either sample.

Instructional Responsibilities

Principle Subject Area. Both UMQ and SIA respondents were asked to indicate the principle subject matter area in which they had teaching responsibilities. Their responses are shown in Table 3. In the UMQ sample, very few (less

Table 3
Principle Subject Matter Responsibility

| | UMQ | | SIA | | | |
| | | | Major Subject | | Secondary Subject | |
	N^a	%	N	%	N	%
Psychology	91	65	79	72	21	19
Psychology & Sociology	27	19				
Sociology	4	3	3	2	21	19
Economics	2	1	2	2	4	4
History, Civics, Social Studies	24	17	19	17	30	28
Biology	2	1	1	1	1	1
Other	15	11	5	5	11	10
No Response	6	4	0	0	21	19

[a]Some respondents indicated more than one area

than 15 percent) report their principle teaching to be in areas outside of the behavioral science or the traditional social studies subjects. The greatest proportion (84 percent) indicate psychology singly or in combination with sociology as their principle subject area.

In the SIA sample for which the form provided for listing major and secondary areas, a similarly predominant proportion (72 percent) reported psychology to be their major subject matter area. In this sample all those who did not list psychology as their major area did list it as their second area. The somewhat greater emphasis on psychology in this sample most likely reflects either the applicants' desire to be viewed as having a clear interest in teaching psychology as a condition for institute acceptance or a stronger interest in an institute among those who identify psychology as their major subject area.

The other subjects most frequently indicated by those in both samples were in the traditional social studies subjects including history, civics, etc. It is of special interest to note the very small proportion of those teaching psychology who identified biology as their principal or even secondary subject area.

Subjects Being Taught. Table 4 shows the numbers and proportions who taught in each subject matter area in addition to psychology during the 1970 to 1971 school year for both the UMQ and the SIA samples.

It can be seen that a fairly large proportion of both the UMQ (56 percent) and the SIA (41 percent) samples had responsibility for teaching only psychology or a combination of psychology and sociology courses. These data suggest that possibly as many as 40 percent or more of those teaching high school psychology teach this subject exclusively or only in combination with sociology. As noted above about 10 percent of the UMQ sample held nonteaching assignments while teaching only one course, psychology. Among those in the UMQ sample who held only teaching assignments, 28 percent (34) taught psychol-

Table 4
Subjects Taught During the 1970-1971 School Year
by those in the SIA and UMQ Samples

	UMQ		SIA	
Subject	*N*	*%*	*N*	*%*
Psychology only	47	34	26	24
Psychology and other subjects:				
Sociology only other	31	22	18	17
Sociology and others	17	12	17	16
Economics	10	7	8	7
History, civics, government, social studies	41	29	46	42
Biology	4	3	2	2
Other	19	14	12	11

ogy exclusively. These figures for both samples are quite close to that (26 percent) reported by Parrot and Setz (1970) from their survey of California high schools.

In both samples the subjects taught in addition to psychology by the greatest proportion of teachers were those in the traditional social studies area, e.g., history, civics, government, etc. Sociology (including social problems) was also taught by 34 percent of the UMQ sample and 33 percent of the SIA sample. In contrast, among the behavioral sciences, economics was taught by psychology teachers in either sample with a rather low frequency.[4] It appears that there is a much more frequent teaching overlap for psychology and sociology than for psychology and economics. These data also indicated that very few of those teaching psychology were also teaching in the areas of biology, math, physical sciences, literature or in the other arts. Frequency differences between the two samples in this respect appear to be reflecting other differences in related factors that will be discussed below.

Characteristics of the Psychology Courses Taught

Course Titles. On the UMQ, respondents were asked to give the name of the psychology course they taught. "Introductory", "General" or plain "Psychology" was the title given by 93 percent of the respondents. For another 6 percent "Social Psychology" was the title used. "Human Behavior" and "Behavioral Science" were the only other titles reported, each by one teacher.

[4] This appears despite the fact that according to the National Science Teachers' Association *Registry* (1970) there were twice as many economics as psychology teachers listed as well as almost 25 per cent more economics than sociology teachers.

Number of Psychology Classes Taught. Table 5 shows the proportion in each sample who taught each number of classes in psychology during a given semester. A majority of those in both samples taught three or more classes with a greater proportion of those in the UMQ sample teaching a larger number of classes.[5] (The difference between the samples for those teaching only one class is somewhat larger if only those with teaching assignments are considered since more than half of those in the UMQ sample teaching a single class are counselors for whom this is their only teaching assignment.)

The UMQ also asked respondents to indicate whether they taught psychology one or both semesters and whether the course was one or two semesters in length. Twenty-three percent reported the course they taught was two semesters in length with 75 percent overall indicating they taught psychology both semesters.

This data indicates that responsibility for teaching psychology makes up the largest proportion of the teaching load for a majority of those having this teaching assignment in these two samples.

Grade Level of Psychology Courses. Table 6 shows the proportions of each sample teaching psychology classes at

Table 5
Number of Psychology Classes Taught

Sample	Number of Classes					
	1	*2*	*3*	*4*	*5*	*6+*
UMQ, %	17	17	17	17	19	14
SIA, %	27	21	21	18	12	1

[5] It appeared that most of those reporting six or more classes were teaching under a modular scheduling arrangement.

Table 6
Grade Levels at Which Psychology Courses were Taught

Sample	All 12	11 & 12	All 11	10, 11 & 12	10 & 11
UMQ %	54	42	0	4	1
SIA %	56	40	1	3	0

each grade level. It is evident that for these two samples psychology classes were restricted almost exclusively to students in the last two years of high school with the majority being taught for high school seniors only. Although these figures do not indicate the relative proportions of tenth, eleventh and twelfth grade students actually enrolled in psychology courses open to those below the senior level, they do appear to be generally consistent with such figures provided by Thornton & Williams (1971) for the state of Florida.

Texts and Instructional Materials Used. The UMQ inquired about the text and supplementary materials used in the psychology course. Table 7 lists the texts with the proportions reporting usage of each. One or more texts were reported in use by 89 percent, with the overwhelming majority of these using one of the editions by Engle and Snellgrove. Nearly one-half the texts used were published prior to 1965, with a majority of these being the earlier version of Engle and Snellgrove. Approximately 15 percent of the respondents reported using texts written primarily for the introductory course in four-year colleges while only 15 percent reported using texts other than Engle and Snellgrove that were written primarily for the high school course.

Nearly two-thirds of the respondents in this sample reported assigning supplementary materials to their stu-

Table 7
Psychology Textbooks Used
by UMQ Respondents

Text (Authors)	Year of Publication	N	%
Branca[a]	1968	5	4
Branca[a]	1964	4	3
CRM, *Psychology Today*	1970	3	2
Engle & Snellgrove[a]	1969	34	24
Engle & Snellgrove[a]	1964	45	32
Hersey & Lugo	1970	2	1
Hilgard & Atkinson	1967	9	6
Kalish[a]	1970	4	3
Ruch	1967	3	2
Ruch	pre 1964	3	2
Sandburg	1969	5	4
Other	post 1965	5	4
	pre 1965	4	3
No text listed		15	11

[a]Written primarily for high school courses

dents. Approximately 20 percent listed five or more items that had been assigned.

Course Content — Topic Coverage. To obtain some idea of the instructional content and relative emphasis within the psychology courses taught, the UMQ asked respondents to indicate the proportion of class time devoted to each of a number of listed topics frequently treated in introductory psychology courses. Table 8 shows this data, as well as the rank order among the topics, with respect to each percentage.

With the exception of statistics all topics were reported to have been included by 50 percent or more of the respondents. Although there was a tendency for some topics in the traditional experimental areas (sensory

Table 8
UMQ SAMPLE OF TOPICS TAUGHT
Proportion of Class Time and Rank

Topic	Topic included		Included 10%+ of time	
	%	Rank	%	Rank
Personality	88	1	56	1
Learning	86	2	44	3
Mental Health	85	3	55	2
Emotion	76	4	17	8
Conditioning	75	5	22	5
Personal adjustment	69	6	35	4
Motivation	68	7	9	13.5
Perception	68	8.5	9	13.5
Individual abilities	68	8.5	17	6.5
Growth and development	67	10	17	6.5
Social or group behavior	65	11	14	10
Thinking, problem solving	61	12	6	15
Social attitudes and influence	58	13	16	9
Research methods in psychology	55	14	13	11
Physiological processes and nervous system	55	15	11	12
Sensory mechanisms and processes	52	16.5	4	17
Measurement of psychological characteristics	52	16.5	4	16
Statistics	1	18	1	18

mechanisms, physiological processes) to be included less frequently than those in the social-emotional adjustment areas (personality, mental health, personal adjustment), two closely related experimental topics, learning and conditioning, appeared among the five most frequently indicated.[6] Somewhat surprising, considering the numbers

[6] Because "conditioning" is usually considered a subtopic within "learning" as a more general topic, the figures, to a certain extent, reflect the same emphasis in two ways.

who also taught sociology, was the relatively lower frequency of inclusion of the two social psychology topics, social attitudes and influence and social-group behavior. This could have been because they were covered in the sociology course. Also growth and development, a topic included in most teachers' own professional training course work was included with about the same frequency as perception.

The differences with respect to topic emphasis do not appear to reflect any similar differential emphasis within the texts most frequently used. The most popular text (Engle and Snellgrove) gives equal and in some instances greater page coverage to topics ranking near the bottom as to those near the top of this list. The responses to this question probably need to be interpreted with some caution since it is quite likely that respondents differed to a fair degree in their interpretation as to what each listed topic represented. There was also probably some difficulty and arbitrariness in allocating content that overlapped several of the listed topics.

Teacher Background and Related Characteristics

Educational Level. Table 9 shows the highest educational level attained by teachers in each of the samples. Although as might be expected no one in either sample held a doctorate, one-half or more in each sample held the master's degree.

A much larger proportion of those in the UMQ sample reported graduate work beyond the master's level than in the SIA sample. There was a similar difference of a smaller magnitude for those with only a bachelor's degree. This

Table 9
Highest Educational Level Attained

Sample		BA BS	BA BS+	Total BA, BS	MA MS	MA MS+	Total MA, MS
UMQ	N	32	29	61	53	25	78
	%	23	21	43	38	18	56
SIA	N	39	15	54	52	3	55
	%	36	14	50	48	3	51

difference may reflect a tendency for those with a better educational background among psychology teachers generally to have less interest in and need for the summer institute program.

Major Area of Concentration. Tables 10 and 11 show the major academic areas in which bachelor's and master's degrees were obtained by those in the UMQ and SIA samples, respectively. It can be seen that the most frequent undergraduate concentration in either sample was in those areas traditionally appropriate and emphasized for secondary education social science teachers, e. g. history, political science or a broad social studies major. Between 45 and 50 percent of both samples had an undergraduate major in these areas. Although psychology was the most frequent undergraduate major outside of the traditional social science area, less than 20 percent of those in either sample had majored in psychology as undergraduates and an even smaller proportion of those with master's degrees obtained them in psychology. Among those holding master's degrees the greatest number in both samples also

Table 10

Major Subject Matter Areas[a] for Undergraduate and Graduate Degrees, UMQ Sample

Major	Total sample (N=139)		BA major				MA major		
			BA only (N=61)		MA (N=78)				
	N	%	N	%	N	%	N	% of total	% of MA
Psychology	27	19	18	29	9	11	9	6	12
Sociology	19	14	6	10	13	17	4	3	5
Economics	5	4	1	2	4	5	0	0	0
History, Political Science	23	17	9	15	14	18	22	16	28
Social Studies	40	29	16	26	24	31	16	12	21
Communication Arts	13	9	9	15	4	5	1	1	1
Counseling, Special Education	1	1	1	2	0	0	18	13	23
Math, Other Sciences	11	8	5	8	6	8	1	1	1
Other	19	14	5	8	14	18	10	7	13

[a]Some double majors were reported for each degree

72   DEVELOPMENTS IN HIGH SCHOOL PSYCHOLOGY

Table 11

Major Subject Matter Areas[a] for Undergraduate and Graduate Degrees SIA Sample

| Major | Total sample (N=109) | | BA major | | | | MA major | | |
| | | | BA only (N=54) | | MA (N=55) | | | | | |
	N	%	N	%	N	%	N	% of total	% of MA
Psychology	16	15	11	20	5	9	3	3	5
Sociology	8	7	3	5	5	9	3	3	5
Economics	3	3	2	4	1	2	0	0	0
History, Political Science	23	21	11	20	12	22	4	4	7
Social Studies	35	32	15	28	20	37	6	6	11
Communication Arts	5	5	3	5	2	4	0	0	0
Counseling, Special Education	0	0	0	0	0	0	15	14	27
Math, Other Sciences	4	4	3	5	1	2	1	1	2
Other	17	16	7	13	10	18	23[b]	21	42

[a]Some double majors were reported for each degree.
[b]Most reported as "Education" without any more specific designation.

majored in the traditional social science areas. Although the number holding master's degrees in psychology is quite small, it should be noted that a modest proportion in both samples hold master's degrees in counseling and guidance. The total numbers holding bachelor's and/or master's degree majors in psychology were 34 (24 percent) and 18 (17 percent) for the UMQ and SIA samples respectively.

The situation with respect to a background in psychology is somewhat different however, if both minor and major areas of concentration are considered and these at both the undergraduate or graduate levels. In both samples there was a slightly larger number who minored in psychology as undergraduates than majored. There were 32 (23 percent) and 23 (21 percent) undergraduate psychology minors in the UMQ and SIA samples, respectively. Altogether including all those doing graduate work nearly 50 percent (68) of those in the UMQ sample and 42 percent (46) of the SIA sample reported majoring or minoring in psychology as either undergraduates or graduates. In addition there was another approximately 10 percent in both samples (12 in the UMQ, 11 in the SIA) who reported being post graduate majors or having master's degrees in counseling and guidance. There were also few in either sample who had majored or minored in mathematics or in the physical or biological sciences.

Course Work in Psychology. The UMQ requested respondents to indicate the number of undergraduate and graduate credits that they had earned in each of a number of psychology course work areas. Although this item was completed by almost all respondents, the fact that quarter and semester credits could not be distinguished and that a number only checked the courses taken precluded obtaining any accurate estimate of course work in terms of either

actual credits or number of courses as such. Table 12
shows the proportions of the UMQ sample indicating
course work at the graduate and undergraduate levels in
each of the psychology course work areas listed. Considering both graduate and undergraduate courses together, the
median number of areas checked was 8 with 30 percent of
the sample checking 10 or more areas and 22 percent
checking 5 or fewer areas.

It is of interest to note that several of the areas in which
the relatively highest proportion of respondents reported
having course work (child and developmental, tests and

Table 12
Percentage of the UMQ Sample Reporting Course Work
in Each Area in Psychology Taken at the Undergraduate
or Graduate Level and the Rank Orders Among Area Percentages

Area	Undergraduate		Graduate		Undergraduate[a] or Graduate	
	%	rank	%	rank	%	rank
Educational	77	1	38	1	91	1
Child, developmental	67	2	28	5	76	2
Psychological tests/measurement	45	4	32	3	66	3
Social	52	3	12	9	60	4
Adjustment, mental health	39	5.5	19	7	54	5
Abnormal	39	5.5	12	10	48	6.5
Learning	26	8	29	4	48	6.5
Counseling	12	13	34	2	42	8
Personality	22	9	22	6	41	9
Experimental	29	7	11	11	40	10
Individual differences	14	11	10	12	24	11
Industrial	20	10	3	15	23	12
Individual mental tests	5	14.5	19	8	22	13
Statistics	12	12	4	14	14	14
Physiological	5	14.5	6	13	12	15
Comparative	4	16	2	16.5	6	16
Sensation, perception	4	17	2	16.5	6	17

[a]Includes those not indicating the level at which taken

measurements and social) were areas that received relatively less emphasis in the content of the respondents' courses (shown in Table 8). The relatively higher frequency of educational and developmental psychology and psychological measurement courses probably reflects the professional education background of most of the respondents although this would not seem to account for the high proportion with courses in social psychology. In general, there does not appear to be a very high degree of correspondence between the course work background of these teachers as a group and the relative content emphasis given in their courses. At the same time the very low frequency of course work in certain traditional experimental areas such as physiological, comparative, sensation and perception is consistent with the lesser emphasis given to these topics in the high school courses.

Summer institute applicants were asked to list on the application form all the psychology courses taken at the graduate and undergraduate levels with credits earned in each and to list those taken in psychology and educational psychology departments separately. Table 13 shows the frequency distribution of the number of different courses taken in psychology departments in response to this item. These figures represent the number of different course titles listed, not the actual number of courses taken which these figures would underestimate. No attempt was made to determine the latter nor the number of credits because of the difficulty distinguishing those that were one or more terms in length and those obtained under semester and quarter credit systems. This figure then represents something closer to the number of course work areas counted for the UMQ sample. The median value for both graduate and undergraduate levels combined for the SIA distribution was about five.

Table 13
Number of Psychology Courses Reported at the Undergraduate
and/or Graduate Levels by Those in the SIA Sample

Number of courses	Undergraduate		Graduate		Undergraduate or Graduate	
	%	Cumulative %	%	Cumulative %	%	Cumulative %
0	14	14	45	45	4	4
1	15	28	17	62	8	12
2	16	44	7	70	10	22
3	14	58	7	77	12	34
4	5	62	7	84	6	40
5	7	70	5	89	11	51
6	6	75	3	92	12	63
7-8	11	86	6	97	11	74
9-10	8	94	1	98	11	85
11+	6	100	2	100	15	100

Because of the diversity of titles given, no attempt was made to classify all courses by specific course work area, however, a count was made of the number of different courses in the traditional experimental psychology areas (learning, experimental, sensation, perception, physiological and comparative) reported by applicants as being taken in psychology departments. Only 7 percent of those in the SIA sample reported one or more courses in the experimental areas as undergraduates while an additional 24 percent reported taking such courses at the graduate level, the greatest proportion of the latter being accounted for by courses in learning.

Although the psychology course data from the two samples is not directly comparable, it does appear that as a group those in the UMQ sample had completed more academic work in psychology than those in the SIA sample. The sample difference in psychology course background is most evident in the traditional experimental psychology course work areas. At the same time however, the figures for the SIA sample excluded psychology courses taken in education or educational psychology departments. This difference is consistent with the UMQ sample including a greater number of psychology majors and a higher proportion with master's degrees than the SIA sample and possibly for the same reason, a greater interest in institute training among those with a weaker background in psychology.

Although it was not possible to obtain a more exact estimate of the number of courses or credits, it does not appear that more than a third of either sample had altogether the equivalent of an undergraduate major in psychology (i. e., at least 30 semester credits in psychology courses). There also appears to be considerable variability in this respect. The data for both samples showed a tendency for those who had responsibility for a larger number of psychology classes to have had more extensive course work in psychology than those teaching a smaller number of classes.

Recentness of Degree and Years Teaching Psychology. Table 14 shows the years in which those in each sample obtained their bachelor's degrees and the highest degree obtained.

It is of most interest to note the relatively larger proportion in both samples who had obtained their highest degree in the most recent years. For those holding a bachelor's degree only, in the UMQ sample almost one-half had received their degree within the two years preceding the survey and almost two-thirds within the preceding four years. A similar trend can be observed for the SIA sample. For those with master's degrees in both samples, more than one-third had received this degree within the two preceding years and close to one-half within the previous four years. Altogether 42 percent of the UMQ and 35 percent

Table 14
Years in which Members of Each Sample Received Their Degrees

	BA (BS) Degree				Highest Degree							
	UMQ		SIA		BA				MA			
					UMQ		SIA		UMQ		SIA	
Year Received	N	%	N	%	N	%	N	%	N	%	N	%
1968-1969	32	24	18	17	30	49	18	33	28	36	20	36
1966-1967	18	13	11	10	9	15	9	17	9	12	9	16
1964-1965	13	9	20	18	5	8	6	11	6	8	6	11
1962-1963	10	7	11	10	3	5	4	7	8	10	5	9
1960-1961	9	6	11	10	2	3	4	7	4	5	1	2
1955-1959	18	13	13	12	3	5	5	9	8	10	9	16
1950-1954	12	9	10	9	2	3	5	9	13	17	3	5
pre 1950	20	14	15	14	5	8	3	6	1	1	2	4
No Response	7	5	0	0	2	3	0	0				
Total	139	100	109	100	61	100	54	100	78	100	55	100

of the SIA sample received their highest degree within the two preceding years. Also, of those receiving their highest degrees since 1968, nearly one-half in both samples were bachelor of arts graduates initiating their teaching careers. These figures must deviate considerably in this respect from those for secondary teachers in other subject matter areas generally.

One of the items of information obtained from those in the SIA sample concerned the number of years they had been teaching psychology and the number of years teaching altogether. The results are shown in Table 15. The median number of years teaching all subjects was seven while the median years teaching psychology was two. It is quite evident from these results and the fact that for 78 percent of the sample the total years teaching was greater than the number of years teaching psychology, that these teachers had responsibility for other subjects prior to teaching psychology. These data also seem to indicate that the courses in psychology were more recent additions to

Table 15
Number of Years Teaching, SIA Sample

Years	Psychology		All Subjects	
	N	%	N	%
1	28	26	6	6
2	23	21	7	6
3	13	12	10	9
4	8	7	11	10
5	11	10	7	6
6	9	8	9	8
7	5	5	8	7
8	3	3	7	6
9	1	1	3	3
10	2	2	5	5
11-12	4	4	10	9
13-14	0	0	5	5
15+	2	2	21	19

the curriculum with a fairly large proportion of them added in the two preceding years, i. e. having been taught for three years or less. It also appears that there has been a strong tendency to assign experienced teachers who have recently completed a graduate program in addition to recent bachelor of arts graduates to teach these newly introduced psychology courses. This might be because the experienced teachers are more inclined to propose or are more available for assignment to teach a new and different subject.

Most Recent Degree Holders. Considering the relatively high proportion of those in each sample who were recent degree holders a further tabulation was made to determine if there were any differences in the educational background between the recent degree holders and teachers having received their highest degree at an earlier date. Table 16 shows the major area of emphasis for those

Table 16

Major Areas[a] of Concentration for Those Receiving
Highest Degrees Since 1968

	Highest Degree							
	BA				MA			
	UMQ (N = 30)		SIA (N = 20)		UMQ (N = 28)		SIA (N = 20)	
Major	N	%	N	%	N	%	N	%
Psychology	12	40	6	30	2	7	1	5
Sociology	5	17	2	10	2	7	2	10
Economics	0	0	0	0	0	0	0	0
History, Political Science	4	13	1	5	7	25	1	5
Social Studies	7	23	7	35	5	18	2	10
Communication Arts	1	3	1	5	0	0	0	0
Counseling, Special Education	0	0	0	0	9	32	6	30
Math, Other Sciences	3	10	2	10	0	0	0	0
Other	3	10	1	5	4	14	8	40

[a]Some double majors were reported for each degree

receiving their highest degree in the two years preceding the survey (1968 to 1970) for each of the samples. Comparisons with the totals shown in Tables 10 and 11 indicate that for both samples, among those holding bachelor's degrees a much greater proportion of the recent degree holders had majored in psychology than those receiving their degrees earlier. (For the UMQ and SIA samples, respectively, the proportions were 40 percent and 30 percent versus 20 percent and 15 percent.) Also, among those in both samples with recent master's degrees, a larger proportion had obtained their degrees in counseling and guidance than was the case for those having received master's degrees at an earlier date. These results suggest a trend toward selecting those with a stronger background in psychology or closely related areas to teach psychology courses.

Psychological Services Provided in Addition to Teaching. The UMQ asked respondents to indicate the psychological services they provided in addition to their teaching duties and whether these were provided on an informal or formal basis. This item was intended to determine the extent to which psychology teachers formally assigned full time as teachers might also be engaged in providing psychology services especially on a regular basis.

Table 17 shows the numbers from the UMQ subsample of 120 respondents holding strictly teaching positions reporting each type of service provided on either a formal or informal basis. Although a modest proportion of psychology teachers became involved in counseling and guidance activities all but a very small number apparently did so on an informal basis only.[7] Among the small number who re-

[7] It is difficult to be sure what this figure indicates, since there are a wide range of student-teacher interactions that might be interpreted as representing counseling and guidance activities. In the absence of any comparative figures it is even uncertain as to whether this type of activity occurs any more frequently for psychology teachers than teachers of other subjects.

Table 17
Psychological Services Provided by UMQ Teachers
Not Having Other Formal Responsibilities
($N = 120$)[a]

	Basis for Services					
	Formal		*Informal*		*Total*	
	N	%	*N*	%	*N*	%
(a) Group testing			7	6	7	6
(b) Individual testing			4	3	4	3
(c) Counseling & Guidance	2	2	27	22	29	24
(a) & (b)	1	1	3	2	4	3
(a) & (c)	1	1			1	1
(b) & (c)			1	1	1	1
(a), (b) & (c)	2	2	2	2	4	3
Total – services	6	5	44	37	50	42
Total (a)	4	3	12	10	16	13
Total (b)	3	2	10	8	13	11
Total (c)	5	4	30	25	35	29

[a]The 19 remaining respondents indicated having formal responsibilities that could include these activities.

ported providing counseling on a formal basis only one did not report course work in this area. There does not appear to be any indication that psychology teachers become involved to any extent in providing psychological services on a formal basis. Among those who held other than full-time teaching positions all reported being formally engaged in provision of psychological services with counseling and guidance being most frequently indicated.

Professional Organizations. In response to a question concerning membership in professional organizations, 37 percent of the UMQ and 73 percent of the SIA sample did not list any professional organizations. Of most interest were the proportions reporting membership in the American Psychological Association which was a nearly identical 14 percent and 15 percent of the SIA and UMQ samples, respectively. Seven percent of each sample reported membership in the National Council of Social Studies.

Professional Journals. The UMQ asked respondents to list the professional journals to which they *subscribed,* while the SIA form asked applicants to list the professional journals which they *read regularly.* A wide variety of periodicals concerned with education, psychology, and related areas were reported with 63 percent of the UMQ sample and 92 percent of the SIA listing one or more.

By far the most frequently mentioned journal in both samples was *Psychology Today* which was listed by 37 percent and 72 percent of the UMQ and SIA samples respectively. The sample difference in this respect probably reflects the difference in the form in which this question was asked of the two samples, i.e. between subscribing to and regular reading of the journals. The *American Psychologist* was listed by 9 percent and 12 percent of the UMQ and SIA samples, respectively, while 6 percent and 16 percent, respectively, mentioned other APA published journals. The only other journal indicated with any frequency in either sample was *Scientific American,* having been listed by 17 percent of the SIA sample although by only 1 percent of the UMQ sample.

Previous NSF Summer Institutes in Psychology. Information was obtained from both samples concerning participation in NSF sponsored summer institutes in psychology. In each sample the same proportion, 17 percent, reported having attended one or more previous institutes concerned with subject matter relevant to psychology with less than 5 percent of either sample reporting having attended more than one such institute.

Discussion

The figures obtained for the proportions of teachers in these samples teaching psychology or psychology and sociology classes exclusively and for the numbers of psychology classes being taught provide some definite indications that psychology (and possibly behavioral science subjects generally) has become a principle teaching responsibility for many teachers. Although it is possible that for both samples there was a bias toward eliciting responses from those teaching a higher proportion of psychology courses, this was less likely to be true for the UMQ sample, for which these trends were actually more pronounced. Moreover, the figures for those teaching psychology exclusively were close to those reported by others (Parrot & Setz, 1970).

The results of the number of classes taught also seem to indicate that where it is taught psychology is a subject of interest to more than a limited number of high school students. This, along with the fact that a large proportion of these teachers had only begun teaching psychology more recently, indicates that there has been a fairly rapid increase over the past few years in the extent to which psychology is being taught. These observations suggest that the main barrier to even more extensive teaching of psychology in high school may be the unavailability of teaching personnel with adequate qualifications.

It is also evident that, for the most part, psychology is not taught as a sideline activity by those having professional responsibility for psychological services in the schools. There were indications, however, that among the full-time teachers there were a fair number with training and degrees in counseling and guidance teaching psychology.

For a relatively new subject the proportion of teachers

not using a text was relatively small, however, there was a fairly high proportion using somewhat older (pre 1965) texts.

The fact that the text that was most frequently used (by some margin) does tend to have a strong science orientation providing topic coverage similar to that of the traditional introductory college text might be seen as reflecting a stronger science, in contrast to a social adjustment, orientation on the part of these teachers. This orientation was not however, as clearly indicated by their reported topic coverage which tended more toward emphasis on personality and individual adjustment topics. At the same time learning and conditioning were science-oriented topics that did receive relatively strong emphasis by these teachers. Topics concerned more with biological aspects of behavior, such as physiological and sensory processes seemed to receive the least emphasis. The latter no doubt in part because the typical teacher in these samples has had a limited background in these topic areas of psychology.

With respect to educational background, it is evident from these results that most high school psychology teachers were trained primarily in traditional social science subjects, mainly history and civics or government. It is also evident that a great majority of these teachers had primary teaching responsibility for other subjects (most frequently those in the traditional social sciences) prior to teaching psychology. It is quite consistent with this data then to characterize the typical high school psychology teacher as one who was trained for and was mainly concerned with teaching senior high school civics and history courses. At the same time it seems reasonable to assume that among teachers in this category generally, those assigned to teach psychology have had greater interest and probably more extensive course work in this discipline.

The clearcut tendency for traditional social science teachers to have responsibility for teaching psychology in the absence of teachers trained primarily in the behavioral sciences seems on the surface to be quite reasonable, at least from the point of view of the general concerns of the subject matter itself. Both traditional social science subjects and psychology have human behavior as their primary subject matter concern, even though the former focuses more on collective action and behavior in a social context. However, an equally good argument could be made for a similarly high degree of overlap in subject matter concerns along different lines between biology and psychology. Nonetheless, very few psychology teachers appear to have been trained or assigned to teach biology. The differences between the numbers of social science and biology teachers assigned to teach psychology courses no doubt reflects a difference in the related factors of individual educational background and interest in the subject matter content of psychology. Another related reason is that it is quite likely that most educators and school personnel tend to view psychology as more of a social than a biological science. It also may be that there has been greater surplus of social science than biology teaching personnel available for assignment to subjects being introduced for the first time. (Some data supporting the latter is discussed below.)

Independent of the reasons why teachers trained in the traditional social sciences are more likely to have responsibility for psychology courses, it may be important to recognize that there is not a very great similarity in orientations or specific content between the traditional social sciences and psychology. That is, there would seem to be very little of the subject matter or of the methodology for gathering the subject matter content of the traditional social siences that has transfer value to the subject matter content of psychology as the latter is viewed by most psychologists. Despite the reliance upon empirical evidence in traditional social sciences there is certainly no concern with experimental methodology and little consideration of objective measures of or relations involving individual differences in behavior, both of these being topics of central concern in psychology. In contrast both the subject matter and methodology of many areas in biology would seem to provide a much better basis for transfer to the distinctive subject matter content of psychology. It would appear then that the actual justification of social science teachers having responsibility for psychology courses does (or at least should) rest entirely on the extent of their background in psychology, as such.

The results obtained from the data summarized above also have some implications for educational programs that would be most appropriate for secondary level psychology teachers. First the results support other indications of an increasing demand for and number of psychology courses at the secondary level. The most recent and possibly clearest indication of this trend is provided by the National Science Teachers Association registry of secondary level science teaching personnel.[8] The registry listings for 1972 compared to those for 1970 for each of the traditional social sciences (government, United States and world history, and geography) showed an overall decrease in total numbers of teachers listed in these areas of 1.2 percent. The figures ranged from a decrease of 6.5 percent for Geography to an increase of 0.1 percent for United States history. These data are generally consistent with other

[8]*The 1972 United States Registry of Junior and Senior High School Teaching Personnel in Science, Mathematics and the Social Sciences,* available from the National Science Teachers Association, 1201 Sixteenth St. N.W., Washington, D. C. 20036.

current enrollment and teacher employment trends. The registry listings, however, show a considerable increase over the same period in the numbers of teachers of sociology, psychology and anthropology in the amounts of 15 percent, 22 percent, and 33 percent, respectively.[9]

If there is a reduced demand for traditional social science teachers and an increased demand for psychology teachers it appears that there will continue to be teachers having their principal training and experience in traditional social science subjects who will be given responsibility for new courses in psychology. With this possibility some consideration should be given to the nature of the educational programs that might be appropriate for these teachers.

In this regard there are several observations based on the above data that seem especially relevant. Considering that the psychology teaching responsibility of a large proportion of these teachers has been a one-semester introductory level course, the psychology course work background of a great majority in terms of numbers of courses appears to be reasonably adequate. At the same time, however, their background in the traditional experimental topics was not as strong as that in other areas nor as strong as might be desired. There were also indications that a relatively stronger background in some topic areas, i.e., those usually taken as part of a professional education program, was not utilized as fully as it might have been. (This may be because such courses tend to focus more on specific applications of psychological principles than on the general principles as such.) Another factor is the fairly large proportion of the more experienced teachers in these samples who had already earned an advanced degree.

---

[9]The number of biology teachers showed an increase of 4.5 per cent from the 1970 to the 1972 listings.

Considering all of these factors, it would seem that the most appropriate educational activity for experienced teachers who are teaching or are likely to teach psychology would be short-term institute programs such as those that can be offered in a typical summer session. Among other things, institute programs can be tailored to the specific educational needs that exist with respect to content and level of instruction in a given area. The most appropriate areas of emphasis for such programs considering the backgrounds of the teachers included in the above samples would seem to be in traditional experimental psychology topics and in empirical methods and logic of science as employed in psychology generally. Although course work of this type is available in a great many institutions, most graduate level courses in experimental psychology and methodology are intended mainly for professionals and are much more advanced and specialized than would be required for the secondary level teacher. Considering the increasing numbers of psychology courses being taught, the need for institutes of this type are likely to be much greater in the future than in the past.

A more recent trend that was noted within the data was to assign psychology courses to graduates with a bachelor of arts degree, having majors in psychology. Although this data did not distinguish between those receiving teaching degrees in a college of education from those having the more typical arts and science college major in psychology, undergraduate programs for the former (i.e., teaching majors in psychology) seem from other indications to be quite rare. This trend as well as other evidence might suggest that secondary level psychology teachers could be best prepared by developing programs within colleges of education for teaching majors in psychology. Considering, however, the frequency with which those teaching psychology are also assigned to sociology courses, that courses in both subjects are typically taught only at the introductory level and that there is an apparent parallel increase in the number of secondary level sociology courses, other programs providing a somewhat broader area of concentration would seem to be more appropriate.

The most apparent alternative would be a broad based behavioral science teaching major which would include rather extensive course work in sociology and anthropology as well as psychology, and it would prepare teachers for introductory level courses in all of these areas. Certainly, if the traditional social science major can adequately prepare teachers to handle both history and civics courses ranging over several grade levels and physical science majors can be prepared for physics and chemistry courses, behavioral sciences curricula could be designed to adequately prepare teachers to handle introductory courses in psychology and sociology and possibly anthropology as well.

The fact that some of the foundation courses typically required in professional education programs are in the behavioral science areas, e. g., child development, educational psychology, educational sociology, should facilitate covering a somewhat broader range of relevant subject matter content than is the case for other teaching majors.

For the same reasons, following the practice in other subject matter areas, graduate level programs for teaching majors in the behavioral sciences could also be developed.

Such a graduate program would seem to be the most appropriate way to provide the necessary background for those trained and teaching in the traditional social sciences who have an interest in teaching behavioral science subjects and in obtaining an advanced degree. At present with few graduate programs of this type, it is necessary for social science teachers with these interests to complete further work in the traditional social science areas or to concentrate in one of the behavioral science disciplines. The former provides little in the way of relevant course work and the latter requires a much greater concentration in a single discipline than is needed for teaching an introductory secondary level course. A third option may be for the individual student to design his own behavioral science curriculum picking what appear to be the most relevant courses from each of the disciplines. Although possibly better than the other alternatives, where it could be done, the latter is pretty much a hit and miss proposition and represents a lack of appropriate educational planning and responsibility.

The development of programs for behavioral science teaching majors should also lead to more adequate and explicit consideration of and preparation in the teaching methods most appropriate for this subject matter content. The kinds of teacher demonstrations, class and individual student exercises, projects and activities that have been and can be designed to convey behavioral science principles differ in various ways from those used in conjunction with traditional social science instruction. Although it may be in connection with this aspect of instruction that the biggest differences exist between the behavioral and traditional social science teaching at the secondary level, there appears to have been little concern thus far with behavioral science teaching methods at the secondary level.

In the past, with a very limited demand for behavioral science subjects at the seconday level, it was reasonable to assign these courses to those having their principal competencies in other higher demand areas. However, the time seems to have arrived when training teachers explicitly for behavioral science subjects can be clearly justified and in fact appears close to being an imperative educational responsibility.

The evidence gathered in this study is relevant to only some of the questions for which information is needed to adequately plan educational programs for secondary level behavioral science teachers. It was also obtained from a relatively small sample which limits somewhat the confidence that can be attached to some of the answers obtained. The following are a few of the additional questions for which more detailed information should be sought to have a better basis for planning such training programs.

1. The extent to which psychology courses would be offered in secondary institutions if more qualified teaching personnel were available?

2. The enrollment in psychology courses relative to that possible at each grade level in schools that are adequately staffed with respect to psychology teaching personnel?

3. The comparative size and socioeconomic characteristics of schools in which psychology and other behavioral science subjects are being taught?

4. To what extent students' educational aspirations are related to their enrollment in psychology?

5. The amount of overlap in teaching responsibilities for psychology and sociology courses in schools where both subjects are taught?

6. The respective academic backgrounds in psychology and sociology of those teaching either or both of these subjects?

7. In what knowledge or topic areas in psychology do secondary psychology teachers feel the most need for additional training?

Answers to some of these questions could contribute

much to establishing the need for and nature of appropriate training programs and activities for secondary behavioral science teachers.

REFERENCES

Abrams, A. M. & Stanley, J. C. Preparation of high school psychology teachers by colleges. *American Psychologist,* 1967, **22**, 166.

Engle, T. L. Objectives for and subject matter stresses in high school courses in psychology. *American Psychologist,* 1967, **22**, 162.

Gnagey, W. J. High School Psychology in Illinois: A 1970 survey. *Illinois Psychologist,* January, 1971.

McNeely, P. Psychology courses in Pennsylvania high schools. *American Psychologist,* 1968, **23**, 589.

Parrott, G. & Setz, G. Psychology in California high schools. *Teaching of Psychology Newsletter,* December 1970, **10**.

Thornton, B. M. A survey of the teaching psychology in the high school. *American Psychologist,* 1967, **22**, 677-678.

Thornton, B. M. & Williams, B. J. High School psychology courses in Florida. *American Psychologist,* 1971, **26**, 1040.

5. *A Survey of the Status of Pre-College Psychology in Florida: 1970-1971*

ROBERT J. STAHL

J. DOYLE CASTEEL

A survey relative to the teaching of psychology in Florida secondary schools was conducted from 1970 to 1971 under the auspices of P. K. Yonge Laboratory School, Gainesville, Florida. The procedures and findings are the subject of this report.

A questionnaire was designed (1) to get a broad range of information and relevant data pertaining to the status of psychology in the secondary schools of Florida and (2) to determine the needs of teachers in the areas of materials and audiovisual instructional aids which they would like to see made available to them for use in their classrooms. In October, 1970, the two-page questionnaire, accompanied by an introductory letter, was distributed to 347 Florida seconday schools. By December 31, 1970, 217 schools (62.5 percent) had returned completed questionnaires.

The survey revealed that psychology as a separate course of study was taught in 140 Florida secondary schools. While 140 of the 217 respondents (64.5 percent) reported that a separate course in psychology existed within their curriculum, 128 of the 217 respondents (59.0 percent) actually taught the course in their schools. This report treats the responses of these 128 teachers as one category of respondents. The remaining 89 respondents are referred to herein as those not teaching the psychology course.

According to information received from the State Department of Education's Division of Secondary Education, 12, 519 students were enrolled in specific psychology courses of at least one semester in length during the 1968 to 1969 school year. During that same year 62 teachers were recorded as teaching these courses. The information collected by this survey revealed that a total of 19,779 students were enrolled in separate psychology courses ranging in length from six weeks to one year with 128 teachers teaching these courses.

The 17,442 students enrolled for at least a one-semester course during the 1970 to 1971 school year represent an increase of 39.3 percent in student enrollment over a two-year period and an increase of 12 percent over the 1969 to 1970 student enrollment reported by those responding to the questionnaire. The 128 teachers represent an increase of 106 percent in the number of teachers recorded in the same two-year period. The degree of increased student enrollment identifies psychology as one of the fastest growing course offerings in the history of Florida education.

An examination of the number of semester hours the 128 teachers had accumulated in psychology and related subjects at either the undergraduate or graduate level revealed that the average teacher of the specific course in psychology had 22.7 hours of college background. Preparatory work ranged from a low of zero to a high of 90 hours with a mode of 12 hours, illustrating the varied nature of the background of the teachers. The average credit hours of the 89 other respondents was 11.7 hours with a range from 0 to 80 hours. The mode of the other 89 respondents (not counting 25 respondents who had no hours of college work in psychology) was 12 hours.

When asked if they felt they had enough college course preparation to teach psychology adequately at the secondary school level, 92 teachers or 71.8 percent of those 128 teachers who responded to that item of the questionnaire answered in the affirmative. Among those not teaching the course but who answered the questionnaire, there was a decided difference in attitude toward feeling prepared to teach the course. The percentage of affirmative responses dropped from 71.8 percent to 53.7 percent, in a comparison of the 128 teachers with the 89 respondents not teaching the course. This suggests that administrators and department chairmen are more likely to let those teachers who feel competent, and whom they feel are adequately prepared teach the course rather than randomly assign the course to any teacher on the staff.

The results agreed with expected findings when the subject area of state teacher's certificates was analyzed in reference to those teaching the psychology courses. Social studies certificates were held by 92 of the 128 teachers (71.8 percent) teaching specific courses in psychology. This far outdistanced the next most frequently marked choice listed as "Other" in the questionnaire which received 16 responses (12.5 percent). This "Other" category included those with certificates in administration (3), physical education (2), philosophy (2), and one each in religion, mathematics, psychology, and English. Guidance and counseling certificates (14 responses or 10.9 percent) ranked third with science (5 responses or 3.9 percent) and home economics (1 response or .9 percent) following in that order. It is important to note that at the time this survey was conducted a teacher could teach psychology courses at the secondary school level in Florida without having had a psychology course in college. The certificate area specialties of the 128 classroom teachers as indicated above does suggest that administrators and teachers alike perceive the course as a social studies or social science course rather than a science course. However, 3 of the 217 respondents did remark at the end of the questionnaire that they felt the course should be a science course. When asked whether the specific course in psychology was offered as an elective or a required course at their school 126 of the 128 teachers (98.4 percent) selected the former.

Information about the grade level of the students enrolled in the psychology courses was sought. At no school was the course offered to tenth graders only or to students enrolled in grades nine through twelve combined. Courses open to just ninth graders or just eleventh graders were found one time each with both of these schools noting that they were new schools and that these were the top grades in each of their respective schools. Courses open only to twelfth graders or eleventh and twelfth graders combined were found in 54 schools each. Thus, 84.4 percent of all courses were evenly divided between these latter two choices. The student enrollment figures reported by the 128 teachers indicated that 15,435 of the total 19,779 students (78 percent) taking the course under them were enrolled in courses open only to twelfth graders or eleventh and twelfth grades combined. Eighteen schools (14.0 percent) offered the course to grades ten through twelve. One possible interpretation of this data suggests that schools and/or teachers consider psychology to be either a college prep or a life adjustment course, neither of which is important before the eleventh or twelfth grades. Another way the data may be interpreted is related to the practice in many schools of requiring certian subjects to be taken by ninth and tenth graders, leaving more freedom of choice to eleventh and especially the twelfth graders; hence, the course is offered to levels at which students may select from among several electives.

In reference to the length of time the course was offered a great variety of responses was received. The most frequent response showed 85 schools (66.4 percent) offered courses one semester in length. The other choices and responses were (1) at least a year (35 responses or 27.3 percent); (2) at least six weeks (5 responses or 3.9 percent) and (3) other lengths not mentioned (3 responses or 2.3 percent). These last three teachers recorded that their courses were either 9 weeks (a minicourse) or 14 to 15 weeks in length.

Further, the survey sought to identify courses or subject areas other than those specifically labeled psychology which contained some psychological principles and subject matter.

In examining the combined responses of the 217 respondents, it was found that subject matter described as psychological in nature was being presented in a variety of other courses and was considered important to the understanding of those subject areas. Courses identified as containing psychological subject matter were the following: sociology (20 responses or 9.2 percent); problems of democracy (19 responses or 8.7 percent); family life (17 responses or 7.8 percent); child development (14 responses or 6.4 percent); contemporary issues (8 responses or 3.7 percent); home economics (5 responses or 2.3 percent) and other (12 responses or 5.5 percent). The "Other" choice included American history, economics, marriage and the family, humanities, and health education. A significantly larger number of respondents (111 or 51.2 percent) did not respond to this item of the questionnaire. There were indications by 65 of the 128 psychology teachers that psychological subject matter was being taught in other courses at their school as well as in their own courses, with 41 of the 89 nonteachers reporting psychological subject matter was being included in their curriculum despite the absence of a specific course in psychology.

Students and teachers alike felt the course was valuable and worthwhile. In schools where specific courses in psychology were offered, 75 of the 115 teachers (65.2 percent) who responded to this item indicated that enrollment and demand for the course had risen over the past two or three years while only 9 respondents (7.8 percent) reported a decrease in demand or enrollment. Thirty-one of the teachers (27.0 percent) who responded indicated that enrollment and demand had remained stationary. When teachers were asked to indicate if the course was considered a popular course for students to take at their school, 121 of the 128 teachers (94.5 percent) answered in the affirmative. One respondent who was not teaching the course reported that although psychology had always been one of the most popular and rewarding courses the school offered, it could no longer be offered by directive of the principal.

Florida secondary school teachers reported that they were in great need of new and various kinds of materials, instructional aides, and information to help them teach their psychology courses. This survey of 347 secondary schools revealed that an overwhelming number of Florida's teachers of psychology desired assistance in improving the quality of their courses. The nature of the responses clearly demonstrated the feelings and wishes of these teachers.

A significantly large number of the 128 psychology teachers used one of the three state-adopted psychology textbooks in teaching their courses. Of the 126 teachers responding to this item, 116 teachers (92.1 percent) indicated they used the following textbooks: *Psychology: Its Principles and Application* by T. L. Engle (used by 86 teachers 73.5 percent); *Psychology* by McKeach and Doyle (used by 25 teachers 21.4 percent); *Psychology: The Science of Behavior* by A. A. Branca (used by 29 teachers 24.8 percent). Twenty-three teachers used more than one of these textbooks in teaching their courses. The textbook most frequently marked by the 89 respondents when referring to psychology textbooks used in conjuntion with other courses to help teach "psychological" subject matter was Engle's.

Although psychology teachers in Florida had these three popular textbooks from which to choose, 49.2 percent of them reported they wanted a new textbook for their course rather than newer editions of the same texts. An examination of the data revealed that while 75 teachers (64.6 percent) reported they used the state-adopted textbooks often or a great deal of the time, 31 teachers (26.7 percent) reported they never or occasionally used these texts. Nearly one-third (31.0 percent) of those teachers reported that they used state-adopted textbooks for lack of other reading materials. Their responses suggest that these widely used textbooks are not including the kinds of topics, information, and subject matter that classroom teachers feel ought to be investigated, explored, and taught in the secondary school classroom. Teachers reported that the texts were either too easy or boring or that they were written for the college level.

Even though in recent years quantities of audiovisual instructional materials and laboratory equipment have been made available for use by the secondary school teacher of psychology, 96.1 percent, or 123 of the 128 of classroom teachers, reported they felt a need for more materials and information to help them do a more adequate job of teaching psychology. An even greater number of teachers (124 or 96.9 percent) indicated they would use these materials if they were made available for their use.

Fifty-one schools expressed interest in beginning a course in psychology at their school, providing adequate information and materials were made available to them. This represents 66.3 percent of those schools not teaching a separate course in psychology. Only seven schools definitely stated they wanted no course. Most of the negative replies cited size of schools and faculty, lack of money, lack of space in their curriculum, and lack of qualified teachers as reasons for their responses.

With the increase in course offerings, student enrollments, and interest in setting up new courses in psychology, the need to assist the secondary school teacher of psychology is becoming even greater. Classroom teachers are interested in improving the quality of their courses and on seeking diverse ways of doing so. Furthermore, this survey indicates that teachers are actively seeking prepared supplementary information and materials to meet their needs rather than continuing to adapt college text materials and popular magazine articles to their instructional units. The findings further suggest that secondary school psychology teachers are currently more humanistic than scientific in their background and objectives and that they are seeking materials to assist them in this direction. One way to respond to the predominant social studies background of these teachers may be to avoid emphasis on materials and instructional aids directed towards the biological or behavioral sciences and to develop materials and aids with an emphasis on social and personal adjustment.[1] A survey of the literature (note the Appendix and list of references) reveals that Florida teachers are not alone in trying to find outside assistance in meeting these objectives.

In conclusion, there appears a great need for educators, scholars, curriculum planning committees, state boards of education and colleges of education to join together to plan ways of providing classroom teachers with some of the materials, information, curriculum guides, instructional units and college preparation they are seeking. Setting up a college major in psychology emphasizing the behavioral sciences, setting up specialized research programs, or establishing resource centers that tend to reach only a small portion of these classroom teachers are not adequate to meet the needs of high school teachers identified in this survey. Since secondary teachers and school administrators perceive the course as being aimed at mental hygiene, personal adjustment, life adjustment and college preparatory objectives, what is *not* needed is a curriculum developed by a committee composed entirely of psychologists and behavioral scientists, requiring extensive (and expensive) laboratory equipment and space, with emphasis on college preparatory subject matter. The various groups interested in promoting a sound secondary school psychology curriculum or course of study must be responsive to the needs of the students as perceived by the classroom teacher.[2]

[1] *Editor's note:* This may indeed be an ad hoc solution. One may also reason that additional training is necessary so that biological and behavioral considerations are not left out of the curriculum by default. (See in this connection Margaret Miller's paper, Chapter 11)

[2] *Editor's note:* The editor certainly agrees that the psychologists and behavioral scientists should not be the only ones concerned with curriculum. The issue of student interest remains complex. The current teacher's perception of student interest may, as was suggested in Chapter 1A be a matter of his predisposition to perceive things in terms of his former discipline area. One wonders how Professor Johnson's students (Chapter 21) who begin their careers with a totally new background will see their students' interests.

APPENDIX
A Summary of the Literature:
Secondary School Psychology

Psychology has been included in the secondary school curriculum since the 1830s. By 1900, it was designated as a separate course with over 12,000 students enrolled. By 1935, its growth had become so significant that the American Psychological Association (APA) organized a separate committee to study its progress.

The 1948-1949 *Biennial Survey of Education* reported that enrollment had increased to nearly 50,000 students. In the twenty years between 1932 and 1952, psychology courses in the high schools grew significantly faster than either sociology or economics courses.

The course gained in popularity and enrollment through the fifties and sixties. Records on student enrollment in 1963 indicated that nearly 200 percent more students were taking the course than had taken it 14 years before. A sharp rise in schools offering the course and the increase in the number of states teaching psychology further attest to this growth. By 1973 it was estimated that nearly 300,000 students were taking the course for credit.

Studies of secondary school psychology courses during the past two decades have tended to substantiate each other. The following list briefly summarizes the important characteristics and facts relative to the status of existing courses:

1. Courses are offered in all 50 states.
2. Student enrollment and numbers of schools offering the course are rapidly increasing.
3. Courses are very popular among students.
4. Courses are more likely to be offered in schools with over 300 students.

5. More schools would offer the course if properly trained teachers were available.
6. Psychology is not required in any state for graduation.
7. Courses are usually assigned social studies credit.
8. Teachers are predominantly certified in social studies rather than psychology.
9. Courses are most often one semester in length.
10. Courses are offered as an elective more often than as a required subject.
11. Courses are most frequently offered during the junior and senior years.
12. Girls are more likely to take the course than boys.
13. Students and teachers see the course as being valuable.
14. There is a need for psychology courses in the curriculum.
15. Personal adjustment and mental hygiene are the two most often stated objectives of the courses.

REFERENCES

Data on the teaching of psychology in the secondary school

Abrams, A. M., & Stanley, J.C. Preparation of high school psychology teachers by colleges. *American Psychologist,* 1967, 22, 166-169.

Alexander, F. Emotional maturity. *Mental Health Bulletin of the Illinois Society for Mental Hygiene,* 1948, **26,** 1-4.

American Psychological Association APA creates information clearinghouse on pre-college psychology. *A.P.A. Bulletin,* 1970, 75, 70.

American Psychological Association. Committee on pre-college psychology: 1970 Committee report (Memeograph), April, 1970.

Anderson, R. L. Psychology in Michigan's high schools. *American Psychologist,* 1965, **20,** 169.

Anderson, J. E. *The psychology of development and personal adjustment.* New York: Holt, 1949.

Anderson, S. B., Ahrews, D. F., Russell, R. & Trisham, D. A. *Social Studies in Secondary schools: a survey of courses and practices.* Princeton, N.J.: Educational Testing Service, Cooperative Test Division, 1964.

Barden, J. I. *School psychology and school psychologists: An approach to an old problem. American Psychologist,* 1968, **23,** 187-194.

Bennett, E. M., Cherlin, D. L., Goldenberg, I. I., Levine, M., & Sarason, S. B. *Psychology in community settings: clinical, educational, vocational, social aspects.* New York: John Wiley, 1966.

Bergeron, R. Psychology in the high school. *The Massachusetts Teacher,* May 1965.

Bernard, H. W. *Mental hygiene for classroom teachers.* New York: McGraw-Hill, 1961.

Bernard, H. W. *Mental hygiene in the classroom.* (Rev. ed.) New York: McGraw-Hill, 1970.

Burgum, L. S. The value of high school psychology. *School and Society,* 1940, **52,** 45-48.

Carmical, L. L. Aspects of mental health in the classroom. Psychology in the classroom. *Psychology in the Schools,* 1969, **VI,** (4), 397-400.

Coffield, K. E., & Engle, T. L. High school psychology: A history and some observations. *American Psychologist,* 1960, 15, (6), 350-352.

Combs, A. W. *Florida study in the helping professions. University of Florida Socail Science Monograph,* 37, Gainesville, Florida, 1969.

Combs, A. W., & Snygg, D. *Individual behavior.* (Rev. ed.) New York: Harper & Row, 1959.

Combs, A. W. (Ed.) *Perceiving, behaving, becoming. 1962 A. S. C. D. Yearbook,* Washington, D. C.; Association for Supervision and Curriculum Development, 1962.

Combs, A. W. *The Professional education of teachers: A perceptual view of teacher prepatation.* Boston: Allyn and Bacon, 1965.

Conant, J. B. *The American high school today.* New York: McGraw-Hill, 1959.

Division Two Committee on High School Psychology. High school psychology and science fairs. *American Psychologist,* 1960, 15,(5), 318.

Engle, M. The stability of the self-concept in adolescence. *Journal of Abnormal and Social Psychology,* 1959, 58, 211-215.

Engle, T. L. An analysis of high school textbooks of psychology. *School Review,* 1950, 58, (6), 343-347.

Engle, T. L. College plans and scholastic standing of students taking psychology in high school. *Bulletin of the National Association of Secondary School Principals,* 1958, 42, 92-93.

Engle, T. L. High school psychology. *Contemporary Psychology,* 1956, 1, 140-143.

Engle, T. L. High school teachers of psychology and APA. *American Psychologist,* 1956, 11, (4), 206.

Engle, T. L. Methods and techniques used in teaching psychology in high schools. *Social Education,* 1955, 19, 346-348.

Engle, T. L. Objectives for and subject matter stressed in high school courses in psychology. *American Psychologist,* 1967, **22**, (2), 162-166.

Engle, T. L. Preparation for teaching psychology in high school. *American Psychologist,* 1960, **15**, (6), 353-355.

Engle, T. L. Some trends and problems presented by the teaching of psychology in high schools. *Psychological Report,* 1955, 303-306.

Engle, T. L. Teaching of psychology in high schools. *American Psychologist,* 1952, **7**, 31-35.

Engle, T. L. Teaching psychology at the secondary school level: Past, present, possible future. *Journal of School Psychology,* 1967, **5**, (3), 168-176.

Engle, T. L., & Bunch, M. E. The teaching of psychology in high school. *American Psychologist,* 1956, **11**, (4), 188-193.

Friedman, K. C. Minneapolis, Minnesota public schools twelfth grade modern problems. NCSS Curriculum Series Number 7 (Rev. ed.), *Social Studies in the senior high school: Programs for grades ten, eleven, and twelve,* 1965, 27-29, 77-87.

Greer, E. *What high school pupils study.* Washington, D.C.: U.S. Government Printing Office, 1962.

Grobman, H. Developmental curriculum projects: *Decision points and processes.* New York: F. E. Peacock, 1970.

Helfant, K. The teaching of psychology in high school: A review of the literature. *School Review,* 1952, **60**, (8), 1952.

Helfant, K., & Jersild, T. A. *Education for self-understanding: the role of psychology in the high school program.* New York: Columbia University Teachers College, 1953.

Hobson, C. J., & Scholss, S. *Enrollment, teachers, and schoolhousing, final report, fall, 1963.* Washington, D.C.: U.S. Office of Education, 1964.

Joint Commission on Mental Health of Children. *Crisis in child mental health, challenge for the 1970's.* New York: Harper & Row, 1970.

Jourard, S. M. *The transparent self.* Princeton, New Jersey: D. Van Nostrand, 1964.

Kohlwes, G. F. The prescriptive educational program. *Psychology in the Schools,* 1969, 6, (2), 183-188.

Leeper, R. R. (Ed.) *A man for tomorrow's world. ASCD Publication from the 25th Annual Conference,* Washington, D.C.: ASCD, 1970.

Liddy, R. B. Psychology for secondary schools. *School,* 1945, 33, 476-486.

Lindgren, H. C. *Psychology of personal and social adjustment.* (2nd Ed.) New York: American Book Company, 1959.

Louttit, C. M. Psychology in nineteenth century high schools. *American Psychologist,* 1956, 11, 717.

Macagnon, V. M. *Social dimensions of the self as an open system: A curriculum design,* Gainesville, Florida; Florida Educational Research and Development Council, 1969 5, (2).

Maslow, A. H. *Toward a psychology of being.* (2nd Ed.) Princeton, New Jersey: D. Van Nostrand, 1968.

Menninger, K. *The vital balance.* New York: The Viking Press, 1963.

Metropolitan Life Insurance Company, School Health Bureau. *Teacher leadership in developing mental health values.*

Miller, G. A. Psychology as a means of promoting human welfare. *American Psychologist,* 1969, 24, 1063-1075.

Moore, T. V. *Personal mental hygiene.* New York: Grune & Stratton, 1944.

Mosher, R. & Sprinthall, N. A. Psychological education in secondary schools: A program to promote individual and human development. *American Psychologist,* 1970, **25,** (10), 911-924.

National Association for Mental Health. *The high cost of mental illness.* (Pamphlet), New York.

National mental health program and the states. (USPHS Rep. No. 629, Revised). Washington, D.C.: U.S. DHEW, 1965.

Noland, R. L. A century of psychology in American secondary schools. *Journal of Secondary Education,* 1966, **41,** 247-254.

Noland, R. L. School psychologists and counselors view the role of the high school psychology course. *Journal of School Psychology,* 1967, **5,** (3), 177-184.

Ojemann, R. H. Incorporating psychological concepts in the school curriculum. *Journal of School Psychology,* 1967, **5,** (3) 195-204.

Patti, J. B. Elementary psychology for eighth graders? *American Psychologist,* 1956, **11,** (4), 194-196.

Patti, J. B. Elementary psychology for eighth graders: Four years later. *American Psychologist,* 1960, **15,** (1), 52.

Periodically Washington, D.C.: APA Clearinghouse on Pre-College Psychology, 1970.

Pietrofesa, J. J. A course in personal adjustment. *Catholic School Journal,* 1968, **68,** (7), 66-67.

Pietrofesa, J. J. Psychology in the high school. *Journal of Secondary Education,* 1969, **44,** (2), 51-54.

Pietrofesa, J. J. Self-concept: a vital factor in school and career development. *The Clearing House,* 1969, **44,** (1), 37-40.

Purkey, W. W. *Self-concept and school achievement.* Englewood Cliff, New Jersey: Prientice-Hall, 1970.

Purkey, W. W. *The Search for self: Evaluating student self-concepts.* Gainesville, Florida: Florida Educational

Research and Development Council, 1968, 4, (2).

Quarter, J. J. & Laxer, R. M. Structured program of teaching and counseling for conduct problem students in a junior high school. *Journal of Educational Research,* 1970, 63, 229-231.

Raths, L. E., Harman, M., & Simon, S. B. *Values and teaching.* Columbus, Ohio: Charles E. Merrill, 1966.

Richards, A. C. Educating for openness to experience: A resource manual for teachers. Dissertation proposal, University of Florida, Gainesville, Florida, 1970.

Ridenour, N. *Mental health in the United States: A fifty-year history.* Cambridge, Mass.: Harvard University Press, 1961.

Roback, A. A. Psychology in American secondary schools in the 90's. *American Psychologist,* 1952, 7, (8), 44-45.

Rogers, C. R. *Client-centered therapy.* Boston: Houghton-Mafflin, 1951.

Schell, J. S. Curriculum for teacher preparation for teachers of elementary and high school psychology courses. *Journal of School Psychology,* 1967, 5, (3), 191-194.

Schneiders, A. A. *Personal adjustment and mental health.* (3rd printing) New York: Holt, Rinehart, and Company, 1960.

Silberman, C. E. *Crisis in the classroom.* New York: Random House, 1970.

Snellgrove, L. Report on American Psychological Association activities concerning teaching psychology in the schools. *Journal of School Psychology,* 1967, 5, (3), 250-251.

Stahl, R. J. *Florida psychology teachers report a need for a-v materials.* (mimeograph) P. K. Yonge Laboratory School, Gainesville, Florida: 1970.

Stahl, R. J., & Casteel, J. D. High school psychology courses in Florida: A status study. *Trends in Social Education,* 1962, Winter, 1-2.

Tanner, D. *Schools for youth.* New York: MacMillian, 1965.

Tatar, C. S. Psychology: A neglected instructional unit in Illinois schools. *Illinois School Journal,* 1968, **68,** 271-273.

Thornton, B. M. A survey of the teaching of psychology in the high schools. *American Psychologist,* 1967, **5,** (3), 185-190.

Thorpe, L. P. *The psychology of mental health.* New York: Ronald Press, 1950.

Trow, W. C. Psychology and the behavioral sciences in the schools. *Journal of School Psychology,* 1967, **5,** (3), 241-249.

United States Office of Education. *Life adjustment education for every youth.* Bull. No. 2, Washington, D.C.: United States Government Printing Office, 1951.

Walker, T. *The mentally ill child: A guide for parents.* New York: National Assocation for Mental Health, 1966.

Wall, W. D. *Education and mental health.* The Hague: United Nations Educational Scientific and Cultural Organization, 1955.

What everyone should know about mental health. Greenfield, Mass.: Channing C. Bete Company, 1970.

Wright, G. S. Summary of offering and enrollments in high school subjects 1960-61. (Office of Education Report OE-24015-16). Washington, D.C.: Department of Health, Education, and Welfare, 1964.

Yahraes, H. et. al. *The mental health of urban America.* (USPHS Rep. No. 1906). Washington, D.C.: Department of Health, Education and Welfare, 1969.

Yeatts, P. P. *Developmental Changes in the self-concept of children grades 3-12,* Gainesville, Florida: Florida Educational Research and Development Council, 1967, **3,** (2).

6. The Chancellor Questions the Issues

A Summary of the Remarks of Harvey B. Scribner

At a conference held on January 10, 1972 at City College, New York, focusing upon issues in the teaching of psychology on the high school level, the audience was fortunate in having the opportunity to be addressed by the Chancellor of the Board of Education in New York City, Harvey Scribner. The following is a summary of the remarks made by the Chancellor wherein he addressed himself to innovative approaches to teaching and teacher training, with particular emphasis on the teaching of high school psychology.

The major focus and emphasis in the teaching of high school psychology should be upon the audience or the students. This is particularly true when developing programs. The needs of the student should be primary. The training and development of teachers should also be directed upon the needs of the learner. Dr. Scribner stated that he was less interested in the technical procedures for certification of high school psychology teachers than in the effects of teachers and teaching upon the student and

Edited remarks presented at the Symposium on Problems in High School Psychology, City College of the City University, New York, January 1972.

upon society at large. Certification should be tied to performance, not "credits".

Chancellor Scribner pointed out that we must concern ourselves not only with the needs of students who plan to attend college and perhaps someday become psychologists themselves, but with the students who will immediately face the crises in society. Problems of overcrowding, pollution and mental illness are prevalent. There is difficulty in interpersonal communication and rampant prejudice and intolerance. How do we prepare students to deal with, cope with and ultimately, to alleviate these problems in society? Part of the answer is to individualize education directly in relation to students' needs and students' ability levels. The student needs to be seen as a unique individual, and needs to be helped and aided when he requires help; not in terms of when the group or class requires help. Dr. Scribner repeatedly stressed the humanistic approach toward education. Far less emphasis should be placed upon the technological or statistical approach.

The humanistic approach should be incorporated into teaching in general and teaching psychology in particular. All too often, psychology is isolated and separated in a particular course. Principles of psychology, particularly those stressing tolerance of individual weaknesses and recognition of strengths should be reflected at all levels and in all phases of education.

Rather than approaching the teaching of psychology from issues such as "do we need a department of psychology," "how will teachers be certified," "how many credits should a particular course be," Dr. Scribner suggested that we must first answer the questions, "what do we want a student to look like;" what do we want a student to have learned during his 12-year experience in public schools. These far more fundamental questions must be examined before the mechanics of teaching high school psychology are discussed. An evaluation must be made concerning what we mean by becoming educated and what the role of the school, the staff, and the students and parents should be in the process of education.

Dr. Scribner addressed himself to the area of teacher certification. He suggested that each of the 31 school districts in New York City should be involved intimately and directly in teacher education programs. He indicated that we have an established pattern for the education of teachers and have remained within that set pattern, whether or not it has been effective. What is required is not a minor modification of existing systems, but a complete and creative change. We must create new patterns. We need within the realm of education, to replace some of the techniques and methods which we already have with something new, rather than continually putting bandaids on the existing structure.

Chancellor Scribner did not attempt to answer specific questions, but rather attempted to stimulate thinking about issues with regard to planning and creating a program to train teachers to teach high school psychology. Considering the discussion and controversy following Dr. Scribner's remarks, he certainly accomplished his purpose.

Section II

Proceedings of Conferences
on
High School Psychology

Introduction to Workshops:
Overview

At the two conferences held at City College of the City University of New York, informal workshops were held. The purposes of these workshops were the following: (1) to allow intensive discussion of specific issues experienced by people "in the same boat," (2) to provide a sharing of experience and a sense of common problem, (3) to foster identity of the classroom teacher of psychology, as teacher and as psychologist and (4) to allow discovery of ways of conceptualizing major issues.

One problem, of course, with this approach is that of rediscovering the wheel. However, to vindicate the workshop approach we need only say that we must build our own sense of movement and of capability to learn. It is natural that any group of educators who assemble to discuss a problem will evolve basic issues which have been formulated before. You may even find such issues set forth in Plato's *Republic:* the issue of learning as rediscovery is not a new one.

The workshops begin a learning process. It is hoped that the reader may join in this beginning, and make this identification of issues part of his own identity struggle.

The workshops presented here involve teachers of high school psychology, persons very interested in part-time teaching high school psychology, persons anxious to work with the high school teacher in an ancillary way, trainers of high school psychology teachers, concerned psychologists who wonder who these "new" secondary school psychologists are and will be, and some State Education persons, who wonder how to categorize (as well as how to help) the high school psychology teacher. In the ensuing pages they will discuss curriculum, teacher training, communication, certification and funding of programs.

In many cases, for the reasons of rediscovery, the editors have tried to maintain the flavor of the search for issues and sharing of experience. Where it was necessary to summarize some main themes, the editors, chosen for their *own* experience and involvement in the high school psychology movement, have attempted to provide the reader with some perspective and analysis of the status of the issues raised.

The Curriculum Workshop is edited by Aileen Schoeppe of New York University. Her joint efforts with Professor Merrifield in establishing a masters level program to train high school psychology teachers has been recently described in the APA Clearinghouse newsletter *Periodically*.

Both the Communication and the Teacher-training Workshop have been edited by Professor Ethel Weiss of City College of the City University of New York. Her innovative work has been in the teaching of experimental psychology to high school students.

The Workshops on Certification and on Funding Programs are edited and analyzed by James M. Johnson of the State University of New York at Plattsburgh. Dr. Johnson's training programs for undergraduates who will enter the behavioral sciences is described in Chapter 21. It is a program that probably will become a prototype and should certainly become an understructure for such graduate programs to train high school psychology teachers as Professor Schoeppe's, Professor Fisher's (Chapter 7) and Sister Mary Keliher's (Chapter 19).

The Workshop on Communication was chaired by Alfred Weiss, who is Associate Professor of Education at City College, and whose particular forte has been creating meaningful classroom experiences for students. His own views are set forth in Part 3.

The Workshop on Teacher Training was coordinated by the senior editor, Harwood Fisher, who is now director of the training program for high school teachers of psychology, at the School of Education, City College, New York.

Dr. William Sivers who chaired the work session on certification problems is the Chief of the Bureau of Psychological Services, Department of Education, New York State.

Judith Kaufman has taught in the public schools and served as a school psychologist. She was Assistant Professor of Psychology at the University of Bridgeport, Connecticut, where she was active in establishing a program in community psychology. She is now at Yeshiva University, New York.

The workshop coordinators were selected in terms of their particular abilities relative to the workshop topics. The coordinator of the panel on curriculum was Sheldon Roen whose study on curriculum is briefly described in Part 2. Dr. Roen, in addition, is President of Human Sciences, Incorporated and has been the guiding force behind numerous publications, which make important contributions to pre-college psychology.

The panel on funding was chaired by James M. Johnson, who is Associate Professor of Psychology at State University of New York. The reader has already been introduced to Professor Johnson's background. He is, of course, one of the editors of this volume, and his own funded program is described in Part 5.

Section II of this book presents a workshop summary at the beginning of each of its chapters. Typically, papers have been selected from the Conferences to highlight major topics or issues raised in each workshop. After each workshop summary, the reader should have the opportunity to hear "one man's opinion," or one person's ideas for implementation. It is hoped that the papers selected will serve this function.

The authors of these papers are in one way or another active in the high school psychology movement, and also their selection is reflective of the general composition of workshop attendees: authors included are high school teachers, teacher trainers and a State Education Department official.

Part 1: Curriculum

7. Workshop on Curriculum: Summary and Analysis

SHELDON R. ROEN, Coordinator
AILEEN SCHOEPPE, Editor

This chapter has a twofold objective: to summarize a workshop, designated to be concerned with curricular problems in high school psychology, which was a part of a symposium held at City College of New York in January 1972,[1] and then to use these presentations briefly as a springboard for some editorial discussion of curricular problems in the pioneer work of incorporating effective psychological instruction into our secondary schools.

The coordinator, Dr. Sheldon Roen, in opening the workshop, set some guidelines for it and introduced the speakers who were to make formal presentations. Sister Hilda Carey described an elective psychology course she has developed and teaches on personality theory for college-bound eleventh and twelfth grade girls at Sacred Heart School in New York City. Victor A. Gallis, who

[1] Symposium on Problems in High School Psychology; Workshop entitled Problems in course curricula, City College of the City University, New York, January 1972.

teaches in Medford High School in Suffolk County, Long Island and who, his paper title suggested, would discuss his thinking on ethical considerations in teaching behavioral sciences primarily described the course he conducts. Dr. Ethel Weiss examined the objectives of the behavioral sciences program. Dr. Marion Brown addressed herself to teacher preparation; because the latter presentation is not directly concerned with the subject of this particular workshop and the topic is covered more thoroughly elsewhere in this volume, it will not be included here.

Initially, Dr. Roen discussed his own interest and investigative work in teaching the behavioral sciences. While primarily focused on a younger age group, his work is most innovative and commendable and his perspective "a broad one"; therefore his remarks are summarized here in some detail.

Dr. Roen sees the behavioral sciences developing in the entire school system as a separate and independent track in the subject areas. He takes as the model for this development the history of how science developed in the curriculum from its original introduction at about the turn of the century.

"If you follow the history of how science got into the curriculum, I think you can see a clearer pattern emerging with what you call the behavioral sciences. Science first developed as substantial subjects of study in the graduate schools where people got doctorate degrees, then moved down into the colleges where science became a very popular subject, and then moved down into the high schools."[2] This is now happening with the behavioral sciences. They are now among the most popular subjects in

[2]Transcription of "Problems in course curricula" workshop. Hereafter in the paper when quotations are not otherwise documented they are from the transcription of the workshop.

the colleges and are moving down into the high schools, at present at least, largely in the separate components of the disciplines of psychology, sociology, and anthropology. Also, at the elementary school level, many teachers in many schools are bringing in behavioral science subjects. Anthropology has already a very strong foothold in the elementary grades, enhanced by the pertinent work of Bruner.[3] Sociological concepts are also quite widely taught, but "psychology is coming in slowly, much the same as nature study came in at the time when science was developing, in that teachers are presenting bits and pieces of the relevant behavior for students to study."

Dr. Roen then described the project he had carried out at Teachers College of Columbia University on teaching children in the elementary grades about human behavior. A primary concern of this project was curriculum. Roen attacked the problem differently from the basic way that curricula have been developed in the past in regard to science and mathematics, that is, looking at the simple structure of the discipline. "We thought that especially in the behavioral sciences and in psychology a better approach might be to try to find out what the kids are interested in and concerned about in the area of behavior because we know that interests develop developmentally." To this end a study was carried out to find out at what age/grade levels children are interested in different kinds of topics. Twelve categories of the behavioral sciences were included — economics, political science and similar subjects, and a number of categories of psychology. Some fascinating data were produced. First, second, and third grade children, especially the first and second graders, are most interested in what achievement is. They are inter-

[3] Bruner, J. *Man: a course of study.*

ested in the phenomenon of learning, how people learn, and why some learn better than others. They consistently picked these areas as things they want to know about, "which is a far cry from what publishers are producing for elementary first and second grade kids." Interestingly, another of the psychological categories, the materials on self, "who am I," was shown to be of less interest to these children. "They had no interest, no matter how you phrase a question, in something related to themselves; they were completely immersed in the industry versus inferiority issue that Erikson talks about and the latency period that Freud describes." There is a very dramatic change in the data for the fourth graders; they are now terribly curious about each other and how one gets along with peers and adults. The topics they are most interested in are social activities and interpersonal relationships. From sixth to eighth grade the data fit a developmentalist's predictions, for the concern there is very dramatically with self — the identity crisis that Erikson talks about. These grades are very much interested in anything relating to themselves and who they are.

Roen evaluates, "On the basis of that kind of research, I think we might have a pretty decent way of thinking about curriculum development, at least in the elementary and junior high school levels, in something we call a natural curriculum." He suggests that comparable data on older adolescents should be assembled and should then be the major determinant of a high school curriculum — what have been the previous learning experiences and what are the learners' interests.

Roen's work surely starts with what seems a most promising, "natural" approach — to ascertain the students' interests in particular facets of the discipline at each developmental stage, and then to tailor the instruction to those interests, concurrently paying attention to the structuring so that knowledge and experience will build on prior knowledge and experience. In this way successful experiences at each level with the subject matter content should nurture increased motivation, increased respect for the discipline and its methods of inquiry, and hopefully, greater self-insight. One can only wish that Dr. Roen would publish these data so this information could have wider dissemination, and also that comparable data could be gathered to include the senior high school level.[4]

In presentation of a description of the course on personality theory which Sister Carey teaches, she invited "instruction" for herself from the workshop participants because " in some ways it . . . makes me very uncomfortable for it violates my pedagogical beliefs."

Sister Carey presented a course outline with an appended reading list; this could be described as following rather closely a historical sequencing of theoretical material on personality, as is done in any academic course. This is described here, but greater emphasis will be placed on her discussion of the students' reaction to the course.

This personality course has two basic objectives: "First, I wanted it to be basically an academically oriented course and secondly, I wanted the students to understand themselves better." The course begins with Freud and Adler and moves on up eventually to Maslow and then to Erikson and other contemporary theorists. More time is spent on Erikson because the adolescent stage and identity crisis "really means something to them and they have a lot to react to there." Time is also spent on Rogers and his description of actualizing behavior. Also, a significant amount of time is spent discussing Skinner's theory. The

---

[4]To a certain extent this was a goal of the Project Talent research, but it did not address itself *directly* to this topic.

current works of Rollo May and other existential and humanistic theorists are also discussed. In a consideration of the deviant personality the work of the British psychiatrist, R. D. Laing, is found to be of particular interest, because the course's emphasis centers on "who is sane, and what right society has to incarcerate people because someone says they're sick or might do something. By this time they've all read *I Never Promised You a Rose Garden.*" As an innovation in the course this year, Lawrence Kohlberg's theory on the stages of moral growth is being introduced. This is being done to show another way of looking at the psychology of the maturing human being, for heretofore there has been no discussion of the question of maturity and growth, except as Rogers keeps coming back to the idea of the evaluative process in a mature person. "Then I think they . . . have enough grasp of some of the general ideas of these theories to start applying them to contemporary problems."

Sister Carey also described some of the course materials. The text, *Living Psychology,* is read, not because it is assigned, but because they like it. Additional reading suggestions are also made. Sister Carey commented favorably on the number of the kinds of readings needed, "It is amazing who will come out with really good articles that help the students to get a better hold on some of these very difficult ideas that are being thrown at them — *Psychology Today* of course, *Scientific American* frequently, but also the *New York Times Magazine, Madamoiselle,* and such." She stressed that current articles on Skinner were especially frequent and used in the course. The supplementary book list includes titles such as *Darkness at Noon, 1984, Brave New World,* and *Walden II.*

Concurrent with the work done in the class, the students are doing individual projects and independent research. "The ones who really want to run mice through mazes can run mice through mazes. They are doing their own exploring, while they are involved in this academic attack."

Sister Carey makes her defense for deliberately omitting some of the traditional topics. "You will notice drugs, sex, and things like that are not mentioned explicitly. This is for two reasons: one, they are getting them explicitly in just about every other course you can mention and two, it is my experience, I don't know how valid it is but it's my experience, that when you bring these things in obliquely the students will not turn you off. If you bring them in directly any adolescent knows that the adult is lecturing and she turns off from hearing it. So I never bring it in directly. But these things come in certainly obliquely in the discussion of self-esteem and identity. But that is why some terribly important problems are left right off this list. They do not mind direct attack on the problems of aggression, of violence, of the erosion of community ties and urban life. They do not mind discussing population density and the effect of the various forms of urban problems, noise, pollution, and so forth as they affect men. They like to talk about self-esteem and what produces it, and identity. Finally, the whole IQ question and what is valid learning interests them."

In her presentation Sister Carey also spells out her dilemmas about the course, how it "violates my pedagogical beliefs." "It is admittedly superficial; it is admittedly dealing with a lot of things that the students could not possibly go into very much at their age. Also admittedly, it is reading oriented, and lecture oriented, which is the kind of education I really do not believe in. The funny thing is, everytime I try to speak out of the role of lecturer, the students put me right back into it. So finally we had, in a true humanistic manner, a heart to heart discussion about this, and I said, 'If this doesn't bother you, it doesn't bother me that I do all the talking and you sit there looking very interested, but I get nothing out of you. So it's okay with me, if it's okay with you.' (But it certainly isn't okay with me.) They said, 'You know these ideas are so new to us that it takes us a long time to digest them, and we just can't react immediately so keep right on talking.' So no more apology for things about the course which I just do not like, but it was designed in answer to very specific requests of the students and this is the way it came out. It interests me that in 1972 a course like this lecture-oriented, reading-oriented kind of a superficial survey would be as enthusiastically received as it is by the students."

Much of the discussion following the presentation centered on evaluation of students in the course. There are no examinations or grades but occasional quizzes. "Some of the students feel that if there isn't a test the teacher isn't serious about it. So I give them quizzes, so that they know I am serious — that is really about the only reason I give quizzes, and they are both quick and painless." Most departments in Sacred Heart school are dropping the use of grades and some have students write out their own evaluations. When pushed further on criteria used to evaluate in this course, Sister Carey said, "The things which I try to mention when I write out the evaluation to the parents are participation in class discussions, not so much how frequent it is, but how much she seems to understand what is going on, how she can apply it elsewhere, the outside reading she has done, and what happened, what I could see was going on in her mind when we sat down and discussed a book. We just talk about the book, then go on from there; it helps you a lot. Really, then, every once in a while, they do a test or a study or something like that."

In her formal presentation Sister Carey touched briefly on informal evaluation of the students' work. She asks each to read one book a trimester from the supplementary reading list; however almost everyone reads more. Her appraisal of what the students get from these readings is very positive and she cites how, with little direction, they see relationships and make connections, even when the readings are fairly difficult.

"What seems to happen is that when we study other people's views on what man is, therefore who I am, they get bits and pieces that hit them hard or say a lot to them. I was absolutely floored at Christmas when one of the students walked into my office and said, 'Do you know what hit me most about all that you've been talking about all year?' I said no, and she said, 'You know that division Freud makes between defense mechanisms and coping behaviors?' I said yes. She said, 'That's a real' — she didn't use the word revelation, I don't know what word she used — ' to me.' She said, 'I watch what I'm doing and I watch when I'm coping and I watch when I'm being defensive and it's really helped me to understand myself better and, you know, I really think it changed me.' And another time another wandered in and said, 'You know when we were talking about Maslow today, you were talking about B-love and D-love, about the deficiency love? I felt as though you were saying it all right to me. You know, deficiency love, that's me, that's the way I am with Jerry, and that's the way I am with my mother.' So these things do give them insights into themselves which very often surprise me." She also reports the school psychologist has had students who, as a result of the psychology class, have asked her questions about behavior.

Another point raised in the discussion period was about sequencing and relates back to Roen's introduction. "This is something we offer in the eleventh grade simply because I have tried it with younger children, and the difference is amazing. On ninth and tenth graders, 90 percent of it is lost and by the eleventh grade something has happened and they are ready for it." Sister Carey also says, in response to another inquiry, that if there were boys in the class she would do the course differently, but does not elaborate how. She also explains in answer to another questioner, touching upon her problem of the students wanting to sit and listen, that most of the instruction at Sacred Heart is done by discussion and inquiry — "the discovery method"; she ascribes the difference in students' approach to the fact that this is the first course in psychology they have ever had.

The personality course described above seems to be the opportunity for a worthwhile, rewarding experience for the girls enrolled in it. One question that persists is one mentioned in some of the discussion but not presented by her: do these students not need a course in basic psychology and a survey of some of the basic research, prior to this course in order to better understand and appreciate this content? Again, the question of structuring and sequencing appears. This question is further a part of an effective evaluation; if there are clearcut objectives for the course might there not be a more formal type of evaluation that would be more systematic and defensible? In fairness, the speaker does stress her experimental approach and some changes she has currently introduced, but a more detailed statement of behavioral objectives for the course would probably help to improve the course and justify the activities included in it. Also, might it aid students' understanding to have theories presented in some academic categorization rather than historically — e. g., the trait theories, the psychodynamic theories, the social learning theories, the phenomenological theories?

The other presentation in the workshop that described actual classroom practice was made by Victor A. Gallis. The title of the paper was "Ethical Considerations in Preparing Behavioral Objectives for High School Psychology Courses," but the presenter commenced by saying, "As usual, my title doesn't have all that much to do with what I am talking about." He also warned the audience then that he was not coming to "any definite conclusions".

The paper began by stating a premise that every effective teacher practices some form of behavior modification and accepts the importance of preparing a set of clearcut behavioral objectives prior to entering the classroom. He demonstrates that in some subject areas this presents little difficulty but suggest that, due to the nature of his subject matter, the teacher of psychology will find his task considerably more difficult. Gallis's rationale can perhaps best be presented in his own words:

"Few would be satisfied with objectives such as: 'the student will be able to list and give examples of Freud's mechanisms of ego defense,' or 'the student will use the techniques of operant conditioning to teach a pigeon to play taps on a xylophone.' While such objectives may well have a place in a particular course of study, they are meaningless unless one finds the means to determine whether the student has achieved the broader insights which may be provided by such activities and whether he can apply those insights to his own life.

"At this point, some may question the wisdom of leading high school students to analyze their own behavior. Those who have but a sketchy knowledge of psychology will often discover imagined evidence of severe emotional disturbance in their own quite normal behavior. Because of this tendency, it is my personal belief that abnormal psychology has no place in the pre-college curriculum. Nevertheless, the student can benefit from examining his own behavior, provided that he is kept from the assumption that the terms behavior and sympton are synonymous. It may be possible for him to recognize and modify those aspects of his behavior that are self defeating, thus improving his ability to deal with the problems he encounters in life. In this way, it should be possible to increase the students' proficiency in personal problem-solving without creating therapeutic situations in the classroom. Yet, we are still faced with the problem of expressing this objective in behavioral terms. How can one measure this proficiency without first establishing a therapeutic relationship? Is it practical or possible to establish such relationships when we must deal with such large numbers of students for such short periods of time? Is it ethical to do so, when so many psychology teachers are not qualified therapists? And when we consider that students come to us not seeking therapy but education?

"Despite these problems, I believe in objectives that will be of personal value to our students. We can do this by addressing ourselves directly to problems that are the product of and pandemic to our social environment, the increasingly common problems of adjustment to what some have characterized as an insane society. Once again, however, we encounter a question of ethics: if we are willing to accept the notion that our society is insane, how can we justify teaching our young people to adjust themselves to that insanity? Would it not be better to become agents of that much discussed but ill-defined counter culture that is alleged to have appeared in our midst? Before attempting to answer such questions we would do well to examine the nature of this so-called insanity.

"Merely glancing through a newspaper should satisfy most of us that we are going through a period of rapid and often violent culture change .... These changes are occurring so rapidly that a great many people, particularly the young, are left with no scale against which they may measure their ideals and aspirations, and with virtually no set of values to guide their behavior. Each day more and more find themselves in a state of functional anomie; that is, we appear to have reached a point where our culture is changing so rapidly that functionally there is no culture at all. Whether one would classify such a state as social insanity is purely a matter of definition of terms, but the problem exists nevertheless. To some this may seem a problem that is outside the realm of psychology. When reviewed on the basis of individual behavior, however, we discover that it is virtually identical to what we know as alienation. When alienation has reached epidemic proportions though, we can no longer think in terms of bringing the alienated individual into the mainstream of society, since the mainstream appears to have diverged into a delta of contradictory ideas and practices. What we can do, however, is to help our students to discover the ways in which it is possible to deal with ambiguity and paradox.

"At this point I am unable to define this objective in precise behavioral terms, since I have not yet developed the simple means to measure a student's needs to cope with ambiguity. But I am confident that such measurement is possible. In terms of strategy I suspect that an experimental approach would prove most desirable. The search for identity is a task that each individual must undertake for himself, but by providing him with the proper tools I believe that we can increase the student's chances for success . . . . One of my basic objectives is to deal with what I call functional anomie and what other people seem to call alienation, for I am attempting to help them to learn to reduce the distances that they create between themselves."

Gallis then described some of his classroom activities, and reiterated that he has been trying a variety of approaches. Two examples, his first and his last, have been selected for inclusion here. (1) "First of all we take away the desks and make a circle of chairs. I have the students just sit there for a while and I tell them, 'Observe each other's behavior.' Of course they become extraordinarily nervous, and you see finger tapping and all kinds of things like that. I go around and I say, 'Well what kind of behavior do you see?' And some of them will say things like: he looks nervous; she looks nervous; she's sitting on her hands. And I say, 'Well, look, there are several people sitting on their hands, and there are some people sitting with arms folded like this with their hands out of the way, and other people with their hands behind them, and some people have got their notebooks on their laps or clutched against their stomachs. What does this mean, what's the meaning of hands, why are we hiding our hands?' And what comes out of this eventually, if you give them enough time, not so much push them as give them time, is that with our hands we tell things about ourselves; hands are a way of communicating and when we're hiding our hands we're blocking off our communication with other people. Then I say, 'How many of you would like your desk back right now?' And a good third of them will admit to wanting their desks back. Then I say, 'Why do you miss your desks?' This they are quick to pick up: the desk is a barrier, it is something for one to hide behind. From there we go on into other barriers, the barriers we create between ourselves and others.

(2) "We get a little into sexual behavior. The nature of touching, what does touching mean. I have two girls sit face to face in the middle of the circle, then I'll say, 'Each of you raise your right index finger,' and they do so. 'Now take your finger, put it on the end of the other's nose.' The reaction you get is the jerking of the hand away and a lot of giggling. So I say, 'O.K., get back in the circle,' you know, taking the pressure off immediately. And if things are really working nicely, I'll have a couple of boys in the middle of the circle, sitting and facing each other. Then I'll have one put his knees together and the other put his knees on the outside of the first boy's knees and press them together. Now this is very difficult to get — you seldom get boys who are willing to do this. Of course we don't force them to do this, just the fact that they won't do it is behavior enough to look at. And from this we can develop ideas that touching somebody has, except in certain socially approved ways like shaking hands, some kind of meaning in our culture, that touching means affection or it means sexual attraction and that boys are taught not to do these sorts of things with each other. This is just a one-class thing, but it gets the ideas flowing, sort of brings out the notion that we really do create barriers around ourselves and why, we feel the necessity of these barriers! I'll stop and, I suppose, get questions, and tomatoes, and things like that."

It is indeed encouraging to this editor that the comments in the ensuing discussion were predominantly of the tomatoes/negative type.

The essence of these was that Gallis scared the students. As the first participant in the discussion pointed out the question of ethics involved what was being done. "If the question is this way it means this, if you won't touch my nose it means this — it is like the Esalen Institute, playing games, and I think it has some of the objections that come of that kind of thing. You are making the kids so self-conscious."

Gallis defended himself: "I try not to take particulars, as a matter of fact, I wholeheartedly try to avoid particulars, that automatically this means this and one kind of behavior means that. The only behaviors I point out are not idiosyncratic, but common to the whole group. Out of this they appear to get some sort of idea that they are similar in many ways, and that the things that they feel about themselves are also felt by other people. Most often I teach what is more of a developmental lesson, and sometimes I'll even lecture because we do not have any kind of reading materials as of yet except for things reproduced . . . . I've had my own anxieties about this to begin with. I sit down in this circle and I am just as tense as any of them. But now that it seems to be working, and I've done it a number of times and had some good results, I feel a little bit more confident with this. I don't think I'd want to take it any further than I've already gone, at least not until I am a bit more sure of myself."

A second participant was even more critical, but in a constructive way: "With all due respect, and I believe you are a very sincere person, I think that you are manipulating. I don't think you have the training; I don't think you have the right to do it. Let me tell you something of my own experience instead of cutting you up, for I do not want to cut you up. You know I have been teaching this for quite awhile and I have five classes; it is a whole year's course. The temptation to do something like this is tremendous; the kids like it but I have waited for I am not trained in group therapy. I think I make a half-way decent psychology teacher but I am not about to start indiscreet stuff I think is dangerous. I really do not think you know where it is leading. I don't think you know what kinds of things you are getting aroused in these kids and yourself, if I may say so."

Gallis again defended himself by saying he did not see that he was constructing the class as a therapeutic situation. "I do not conduct therapy sessions, I conduct experiments. I only deal with observable behavior, and in order to do this effectively I have to create artificial conditions which make certain behavior patterns easier to observe, just as if I were teaching operant conditioning."

Another inquired, "Within your framework would you discuss with the students any possible advantages to these social barriers?" Some of this exchange is also best given verbatim.

"Definitely yes. The advantages to some barriers become obvious almost immediately. In fact, you know I personally refuse to delve into any particular student's problems." After giving several examples, he concludes, "But because I do not delve into them personally, I am not attacking their defenses so much as I am demonstrating that the defenses exist."

The questioner repeated, "My question really was whether you pick up both, not only the disadvantages of defense mechanisms, but the advantages."

"Yes, we get into a more formal approach when we start listing defense mechanisms. I have never found two lists that agreed with each other. But just talking about defensive behavior in general, I have always sort of asked when can this kind of behavior be good for you, when can it be adaptive, when can it help you."

Another participant asked Gallis to comment on his idea that abnormal psychology does not belong in the high school curriculum. He replied that his personal approach, and the only interpretation he presents to his class, is that of Dr. Thomas Szasz. "I work on the idea that there's a range of behavior and that some behavior occurs more often than other behavior but that we just do not make value judgements concerning it." He has also reproduced an article on Szasz from the *New York Times Magazine* (Scarf, 1971).

Three years ago, in reporting on a similar conference, this editor stated she was "very concerned about the number of suggestions for sensitivity training, encounter groups, and such. The danger inherent in such activity, particularly when carried on by those without great specialized training is incalculable and many participants are evidently not fully aware of this. Such activity does not properly fit in any high school psychology course, as we envision it." (Merrifield and Schoeppe, 1970). If anything, these convictions are even stronger today! Whether such groups should be a part of the programs of secondary schools under some other aegis is another matter, *but they should not be looked upon as appropriate content in a formal psychology course for numerous reasons,* in addition to the qualifications of the teacher for conducting them.[5]

A major consideration goes back again to the developmental sophistication of the learners. The writer likens the situation to the innumerable times she encountered students in general psychology courses who had read much of Freud and could enthusiastically quote him, but they

---

[5]*Editor's note:* Gallis comments: "I do not attempt to practice group therapy in the classroom, and must *insist* that this be made perfectly clear. My experiments are intended to be and function as learning experiences, and are in no way cathartic or therapeutic. At my school, more "therapy" goes on in hygiene classes than I would ever allow in my psychology classes."

could not define the term "psychology." What the students need is an understanding of some basic concepts and definitions and an appreciation of the methods by which these were derived! The editor would suggest that if this were the course content, there would be little need for much concern about ethics. A further suggestion is that the discipline does have a common definition of most terms and that it might enhance a learner's self-esteem to know these. For example, there is agreement on the most common defense mechanisms; also, there are quite simple measures of tolerance for ambiguity.

This editor is also upset by the absence of any kinds of objective appraisal. "It seems to be working" and "had some good results" are not sufficient to satisfy. One would like more evidence on the "behavior modification" in students.

Coincidentally, Robert C. George has been concerned in much the same way about youth and their problems. He established and coordinated the Worcester Crisis Center, a drug-oriented hotline servicing central Massachusetts. Conversations with these troubled youth reinforced his personal belief that a serious gap existed between the traditional academic curriculum and the interests of young people. "As a psychology teacher I realized the need for a course that would help bridge the gap between school and the ego-identity problems of youth." (George, 1973). With this thought in mind George attempted to "create a psychology curriculum which creatively addresses those issues which loom large in young peoples' lives. The quest for identity, generation gap, alienation, growing up in different cultures, and adolescence are examined via cognitive and affective pedagogical techniques." (George, 1972). This course, first developed in 1970, is currently being used in eight Massachusetts high schools and initial feedback from both teachers and students has been very positive. One session at the 1972 meetings of the National Council for the Social Studies was devoted to the discussion of the course and an article describing this curriculum in some detail is in the January, 1973 issue of *Social Studies*. Readers are referred to this account of this well-developed program.

In examining the two programs described in the Workshop, attention is called to the fact that in many ways the approaches are complete opposites. It is true that the students represent very different groups — at Sacred Heart all are college-bound while in the other school only about 18 percent will attend college. But the question persists: if all these young people are striving for self-insight and concerned with ego-identity, might it not be possible to have some greater commonality in their educational experiences?

It is indirectly to this question that Dr. Weiss[6] addressed herself in her presentation when she spoke about objectives for a high school psychology course and the relevance of what is being done in these courses. She warned that her presentation was "very much colored by the fact that the center of the world is really very much psychology." She described the two antithetical approaches: that often advanced by the secondary teacher for a mental health or adjustment approach and the demand by the academic psychologist that the approach be rigorously scientific; then she suggested that both do a disservice to both the student and the discipline. The disadvantage of the mental hygiene approach in the secondary school can be three-

---

[6]*Editor's note:* Professor Weiss' paper is presented in its entirety, following this workshop summary (Chapter 9). Her remarks are included in some detail, here to maintain the nature of this workshop's themes and interactions.

fold: (1) it holds out a false promise of adjustment made easy, (2) values and data readily can become inappropriately intertwined and (3) the student can easily develop a very distorted idea of what the purposes and practices of psychology are. "In addition such courses are too often used by students as constant gripe sessions and an easy grade." On the other hand, the rigorous, scientific course can fail as readily but for very different reasons. It can be readily dismissed as (1) irrelevant, (2) too difficult and (3) misleading in not fulfilling the implicit promise of any course called psychology. Neither course succeeds in informing and involving the students; neither can be done effectively without the other. Dr. Weiss then proposed that "the proper objective of the secondary school psychology course be an appreciation of how psychology as a scientific discipline tries to understand people and the facts that influence how people feel, think and behave. If this overall objective is agreed upon, it then seems to me to follow that the particular content chosen to illustrate the basic way in which psychologists function becomes totally immaterial. There is no reason that it cannot be selected from areas of immediate concern to the student, in fact, more positively it can be stated that the particular content should be chosen from the areas of student concern." Such material holds a terrific interest and the problems of motivating the student become minimized. In addition, the quest for relevancy has been met. Dr. Weiss defended that this approach is not a "vulgarization" of psychology, if, as she stated, the material used is shaped and directed to certain specifics. "Psychology is an empirical discipline that uses the correlational and experimental methods to answer questions. Psychology as an empirical discipline does not have truth; it is an ever-increasing, never attainable approximation to truth." The goals Dr.

Weiss stresses would be to help the student understand how psychologists try to formulate and answer psychological questions. In order fully to communicate this approach it is necessary, at least in part, to be able to apply the scientific method to answer some questions within the realm of the students' experience, and then to go beyond the students' current view. But in order to do so it is necessary to start with their view. Dr. Weiss gives several illustrations to clarify this approach. She uses one, "the issue of the status of astrology as a method used by avant-garde people", as a topic that could be used to illustrate the importance of suggestion and a need for blind control and a scientific method to test a hypothesis. She also discusses several memory experiments, stressing always the methodology that would produce a tentative answer. She suggests television ads can be fruitfully used to illustrate what one may want to know about the underlying processes. "I get excited about aspirin claims, or cold medicines. Do brand X aspirins really cure headaches? How do we know that it is brand X, or that the headache did not go away by itself? Does this make a difference in our behavior? I think that by going through something practical from their own experience you can get at the importance of analysis. With a more sophisticated class, and perhaps a more interdisciplinary one, we can look at juvenile delinquency or cultural deprivation differences and ask more abstractly how does the underlying function determine our analysis of the problems . . . . At the end of the first psychology course, the student should have an idea of how the psychologist formulates questions and how he would try to answer them. The student should have an idea of the provisional nature of the answers offered."

A participant suggested that high school students are

aware that there are many psychologists and psychologies competing for attention and questions will be raised about Freud and Rogers and so on. The suggestion is made that on the high school level we have to go beyond emphasis on a single technique or approach to psychology because "these are the questions they put to you, they do not buy your expertise, they are suspect about the value in your field and you have to face that question."

To this Dr. Weiss replied, "I think that there is a very legitimate humanistic approach that is sort of different from the one that I am comfortable with, but certainly much of our data in psychology is a correlation of experimental field data. However, I think that the value of the experimental method really goes beyond a particular approach because questions raised from the humanistic perspective can be answered by some application of these methods." "But then you are teaching a method of thinking." "That is what was my concern."

Perhaps this last exchange represents what constitutes a very real problem in secondary school psychology today. That is one of the conclusions reached by Dr. James J. Ryan from his analysis of data recently gathered from 248 respondents who were either teaching secondary school psychology in one of four upper Midwest states or were applicants for a National Science Foundation summer institute for secondary psychology teachers. (Chapter 4)

The development of programs for behavioral science teaching majors should also lead to more adequate and explicit consideration of and preparation in the teaching methods most appropriate for this subject matter content. The kinds of teacher demonstrations, class and individual student exercises, projects, and activities that have been and can be designed to convey behavioral science principles differ in various ways from those used in conjunction with traditional social science instruction. Although it may be in connection with this aspect of instruction that the biggest differences exist between the behavioral and traditional social science teaching at the secondary level, there appears to have been little concern thus far with behavioral science teaching methods at the secondary level. (Ryan, 1972).

Several other problems seem to stand out from this workshop. One cannot help but be impressed by the almost total lack of any reference to the materials that have been developed expressly for use in secondary psychology courses. (Sister Carey's use of *Living Psychology* as a text is the sole exception.) Also, there is no mention of any of the professional materials recently developed under the auspices of the American Psychological Association, nor of its Clearinghouse.[7] One wonders if they were unknown to the speakers, inadvertently omitted, or ill-regarded! Nor is there mention of any of the other available professional literature.

Another serious problem seems to be the lack of any systematic effort to evaluate the courses, and, more frightening, seemingly no real awareness that this constitutes a serious problem.

There are, and have been for many years, guidelines for developing curricula. These vary, but generally all include similar steps:

1. Defining the behavioral objectives for the curriculum — i. e., what you wish the learners to be able to do after these experiences that they were not able to do before. Objectives need to consider the needs of the learner, the needs of the society, and the needs of the discipline.

[7]*Periodically; Program on the teaching of psychology in the secondary school: Final Report;* curricular units developed by R. A. Kasschau and by B. S. Markman.

2. Determining what learning activities can be used to accomplish the necessary behavioral changes and how these can best be organized to do this.
3. Assessing the "readiness" of the learner to succeed in these activities. This needs to take account of his potential, his previous learning experiences so he will have developed the requisite skills, and his motivations.
4. Designing some plan for evaluating how well the stated behavioral objectives have been achieved.

Many curriculum books (cf. Taba, 1962; Gwynn and Chase, 1969; N.S.S.E. Yearbook, 1971) discuss various rationale for curricula planning. It would seem some of these need much wider usage.

At one point, Roen, in discussing the hidden curriculum, suggests, "We are going to have to become explicit about what it is we think we are doing." This seems a crying need, and with it an assessment of what is being accomplished. It is hoped that the American Psychological Association's proposed five-year project on development of instructional modules for secondary school behavioral and social science instruction (Hunt, *et al.* 1972) will move us much closer toward that desired end of greater clarity about the objectives of secondary school psychology and appropriate activities for reaching those goals.

REFERENCES

Bruner, J. *Man: A course of study.* Newton, Massachusetts: Educational Development Center (EDC), 1967.

George, R. C. Personal communication, 1972.

_____. A new approach to high school psychology. *Social Studies,* **64,** Jan. 1973, pages 20-25.

Gwynn, J. M. and Chase, J. B., Jr. Curriculum principles and social trends, 4th edition. New York: Macmillan, 1969.

Hershey, G. L. and Lugo, J. O. *Living psychology: An experiential approach to behavior.* New York: Macmillan, 1970.

Hunt, R. G., Davol, S. H. and Schoeppe, A. *Proposal for precollege psychology and behavioral science.* Washington, D. C.: American Psychological Association. Ms. No. 124, Journal Supplement Abstract Service.

Merrifield, P. R. and Schoeppe, A. Report of psychology for youth: Conference for high school teachers of psychology. New York: New York University, 1970.

National Society for Study of Education. *The curriculum: Retrospect and prospect.* Seventieth Yearbook. Chicago: University of Chicago Press, 1971.

Ryan, J. J. A survey of high school psychology: Teacher and course characteristics. Mimeo paper, 1972.

Scarf, M. Normality is a square circle or a four-sided triangle. *New York Times Magazine,* October 3, 1971.

Symposium on problems in high school psychology: Workshop on problems in course curricula. Transcription, 1972.

Taba, H. *Curriculum development: Theory and practice.* New York: Harcourt, 1962.

8. High School Psychology in Practice: A Field Approach

IRA LIPTON

In September 1971, Jamaica High school in New York City introduced an elective course in psychology, which has since become one of the most popular courses in our school. In the previous term, the students voted that psychology and a number of electives should be offered to students in their senior year. The elective has now been expanded to a minicourse in the behavioral sciences, and both electives can be requested by any student at our school.

The syllabus of the course, as set out below, includes a wide variety of areas and five major units throughout the term:

Unit I: Psychology—A Behavioral Science
Unit II: The Learning Process
Unit III: Patterns of Behavior
Unit IV: Mental Health
Unit V: Group Behavior and Social Dynamics

Prepared in part for the Symposium on Problems in High School Psychology, New York, City University, January 1973.

149

SYLLABUS: INTRODUCTION TO PSYCHOLOGY

Unit I: What is Psychology — A Behavioral Science
   A.   Definition of Terms — relation to other
        sciences
   B.   Aims and Goals of Psychology
   C.   Professions in Psychology
   D.   Methods of Research in Psychology

Unit II: The Learning Process
   A.   Study Skills — Inventory
   B.   Learning Theories — conditioning — classical
        to present percent — B. F. Skinner
   C.   How to increase learning efficiency (transfer of
        learning, etc.)

Unit III: Patterns of Behavior
   A.   Motivation
   B.   Emotions — Development Description
   C.   Intelligence
        (1) Wechsler Adult Intelligence
        (2) Test for ghetto children
        (3) I.Q. testing N.Y.C. Board of Education
        (4) Hereditary vs. Environment

   D.   How does Behavior Develop — Administration of
        of Strong Vocational Interest Inventory
   E.   Theories of Personality Development — Freud,
        Erickson, Jung, Horney

Unit IV: Mental Health
   A.   Mental Health Inventory
   B.   Emotional Problems of High School Students
   C.   Mental Illness — Behavior pathology

(1) Abnormality? Normality
(2) Neuroses
(3) Self Defense Mechanisms
(4) Psychosis
(5) Additional Behavior Disorders
(6) Addiction — Films — State Narcotics
(7) Causes of mental illness — environment and
heredity
D.   Therapy — Behavior Modification — Description
of psychotherapy, shock therapy, psychodrama,
etc.
E.   Psychology in the Community

Unit V: Group Behavior & Social Dynamics
A.   Influence of the family on group behavior.
B.   Intergroup relations
C.   Social Attitudes & Social Problems
(1) formation of attitudes & prejudices
(2) communications & collective behavior
D.   Human Relations Sensitivity
Requirements:
A.   Term paper in area of psychology
or completion of field work experience.
B.   Basic Text - Munn, *Psychology*
C.   Outside reading

The textbook used is Munn, Fernald, & Fernald, *Basic Psychology,* which is an adaptation of their longer text. I have found this text to be an adequate source of general information written at a level for the average and above average high school student. Additional paperback books provide supplementary source material. A recent publication, Annual Editions Readings in Psychology '72-'73 — Dushkin Publishing Group, has proved to be a highly motivating and exciting source of information of current articles for introductory psychology.

Our students were offered the alternative of completing

a field work experience or a term project. A term project could either be a term report or a slide presentation that included prisons or schools for the mentally retarded. However, the majority of our students selected a fieldwork experience, which included working after school or on the weekend in a variety of institutional settings. Some of our students are now completing volunteer work at the Creedmore State Hospital (Queens Children's Hospital), the United Cerebral Palsy at Jamaica, Jamaica's Childrens Shelter, and the public schools in our community. Of all the experiences in our course, I have found the students who selected the fieldwork experience to have profited by an invaluable experience that has influenced many of them in career decisions in the social services. Many of the students were fortunate enough to have worked with occupational therapists, psychologists, psychiatric social workers, and teachers who worked with autistic, brain-damaged, physically handicapped, and emotionally disturbed children. The student reaction to this experience was always positive; however, working with these children was not the easy task they thought it would be. I recall that one of our students was given a young, autistic child to work with during parent hour (this particular child never received visitors). The student brought the child a chocolate cup cake as a sort of friendly offering by way of introducing herself. The cake was promptly smashed over her head as the child attempted to bite our volunteer student. Our student told me of the incident the next day and began to cry, saying that she would no longer continue at the hospital. I asker her if she would reconsider and if she would return for just one additional week, which she agreed to. She not only continued the next week but worked with the child for six months after the completion of our course, when she entered college.

As I now return to many of these institutions for a second year, I am surprised and delighted to find students who are still working there voluntarily between classes from the local college campuses. Some unexpected but amusing incidents occurred from time to time. Two of our female students, when working with two retarded young boys, were asked by them to disrobe; and they found the boys to be quite precocious in other areas.

One of our students named Michael was most effective in working with children who had cerebral palsy. He seemed to feel that working with crippled children gave him a sense of empathy and confidence. The supervisors at the Center insisted on writing college recommendations for Michael, and the counselors at school noticed a much more positive self-image in Michael. He became the Center's first black Santa Claus and Easter bunny, and was asked to appear on the National Cerebral Palsy Telethon. Many of our black students were especially interested in working at the Children's Shelter since a majority of these children were of minority background. They enjoyed working with and helping these youngsters and tutored the ones who required such assistance. Many of these students by way of explanation to their classmates, told of the effects of institutional living and homelessness of these children.

I recently read a study in *Psychological Abstracts* (June 1970, Vol. 44) that was completed in the Soviet Union. The study presented an analysis of the results of a questionnaire on what is personally looked for in choosing a vocation. Comparison with a similar questionnaire and material in the United States showed that young Americans view vocations in terms of protection of personal well-being and material security, whereas Soviet youth's perception of values emphasizes benefits to society and prospects of creative growth. Perhaps we in secondary education do not give our students the exposure to those areas that benefit society in a humanistic way. Not all of my students will major in special educaion or some related area, but I believe all have profited by a practical experience they could never understand by simply reading a book. The students reaction to the fieldwork program was always enthusiastic, and for many of them it was their first opportunity to practice their idealism.

9. Should High School Psychology
Be Relevant?

ETHEL WEISS

What is the appropriate goal of a secondary school psychology course? There is extensive documentation of the disagreement between secondary school teachers and psychologists in answer to this question. Secondary school teachers tend to see the focus of this course as being adjustment and self-understanding. Psychologists tend to emphasize the scientific rigor of the discipline. Both approaches probably do a disservice to the student and the discipline.

The disadvantage of the mental hygiene approach to secondary school psychology can be threefold (1) it can hold out false promises of "adjustment made easy", (2) values and data can become inappropriately intertwined and (3) the student can easily develop a very distorted idea of what the purposes and practices of psychology are. In addition, such courses are too often viewed by students as contentless gripe sessions and an easy grade.

The rigorous scientific course can fail as readily with the students as the mental hygiene course but for very different reasons. Because of its abstraction, it can be dismissed as (1) irrelevant, (2) too difficult and (3) misleading in not fulfilling the implicit promise of any course called psychology to teach one about oneself.

Paper prepared especially for Symposium on Problems in High School Psychology, City College of the City University, New York, January 1972.

For different reasons both these approaches are ineffective. Neither course succeeds in both involving and informing the student. Neither can be done effectively without the other. How can the relevance of one and the rigor of the other be combined? The answer is very simple, providing certain assumptions are made. These assumptions involve agreement as to the appropriate goals of a secondary school psychology course as well as a commitment to the preparation of teachers prepared in the discipline.

I wish to propose that an appropriate objective of the secondary school psychology course be an appreciation of how psychology as a scientific discipline tries to understand people and the factors that influence how people feel, think and behave. If this overall objective is agreed upon, it then seems to me to follow that the particular content chosen to illustrate the basic way in which psychologists function becomes immaterial. Since the content, per se, is not particularized, the content should be chosen from areas of student concern. Such material is of intrinsic interest to the student and the problems of motivating the student become minimized. In addition the quest for relevancy has been met.

Isn't this approach a vulgarization of psychology? No! It would be if we stopped with the selection of relevant content; it isn't if the material used is shaped and directed to certain specifics.

What are these specifics? I suggest that they are the empirical nature of psychology. Psychology is an empirical discipline that uses the correlational and experimental methods to answer questions. Psychology as an empirical discipline does not have truth, but is an ever-increasing, never attainable approximation to truth. My goal for the course would be to help the student understand how psychologists try to formulate and answer psychological questions. In order to fully communicate this approach, it is necessary at least in part to be able to apply the scientific method to answer some questions within the realm of the student's experience. Again, this is not the goal; but in order to go beyond the student's current view, it is necessary to start with where he is currently.

What kinds of questions might come up and how can they be used to educate the student? Let us take for an example the topical issue of the status of astrology as a method of finding out about people. This topic could be used to illustrate the importance of suggestion and the need for a blind control as well as the utility of the correlational method for testing hypotheses. How abstractly one handles the principles involved will depend on the level of the student, but even with a very mediocre class certain principles can be illustrated. Students can be asked to bring in astrological descriptions from the newspaper, which can be read with the correct designation, e. g., Scorpios are loving, Capricorns are friendly, etc.. A table can be made (perhaps partitioned further into believers and nonbelievers) indicating whether the description for the student's own month is more likely to be "true" or accurate than description of people of other "signs." Similar information without the correct month indicated until after the student has picked out the ones that are or aren't appropriate to him might yield very different results. An interesting discussion can develop on how we ordinarily validate expectations, on the need for controls, on selective attention, or memory distortions. The initial starting point may lead to a discussion of many different topics. The incidential discrediting (or at least doubt raising) of astrology is purely a bonus!

A correlational or naturalistic study might nicely be

followed by an experiment. Perhaps we pick up on the question of memory distortion. The old game of telephone or rumor can be played. One half the class passes on an aural message the other half the same message written. Various questions suggest themselves: What has to be constant? (The message and the time for the communication) Why? What's the difference in outcome as a function of the two conditions? What does this tell us about some "memory" distortion? (That the problem is, at least in part, an input problem.)

Why do we try to analyze these things? What is the consequence of knowing about underlying processes? Here television ads can be used to suggest why we want to know about underlying processes. Does Brand X aspirin really cure headaches? How can we know? What difference does it make if our attribution is correct or not - the headache is gone?

With a more sophisticated class and perhaps a somewhat more interdisciplinary focus, we can look at juvenile delinquency or cultural deprivation (differences) and ask more abstractly, how does the underlying assumption determine the cures we recommend and the controls we use.

Psychologists raise interesting questions and have exciting ways of trying to find the answers to their questions. At the end of the first psychology courses the student should have an idea of how a psychologist would formulate a question and how he would try to answer it. The student should have an idea of the provisional nature of the answers offered. Hopefully, in addition, the student has become aware of the fact that we live in a problematic world with ever-receding horizons, and that the unknown is a vaster terrain than the known.

Part 2: Communication with Students

10. Workshop on Communication with Adolescent Students

ALFRED WEISS, Panel Coordinator
ETHEL WEISS, Editor

This chapter's objective is to present a summary of the workshop concerned with problems in communicating with the adolescent student. The editorial discussion of the issues raised in this workshop will be presented later in this section of the book. After the workshop summary, the views expressed by the coordinator of the panel are amplified in Professor Alfred Weiss' paper. Discussion of some of the differences in his views and those in Margaret Miller's paper which follows may serve to crystallize the workshop issues.

The panel was chaired by Professor A. Weiss. He stated that the goal of the session was to generate some principles of communication that would be useful in relating to the students.

The first participant said that when he thought of communication he didn't think of it on a verbal level. He thought of it on a nonverbal level, as a smile, as a touch, a pat on the back. Another participant expressed agreement,

Symposium on Problems in High School Psychology; Workshop entitled Communication with Adolescent Students. City College of the City University, New York, January 1972.

indicating "It's nice to be friendly. You are communicating and then they begin to tell you their problems." But she pointed out, she is not a therapist. She cannot meet with students continuously and she was not trained to help them and really solve problems fundamental to their lives. She found it very upsetting not to have adequate places to send these kids, and not to have facilities for treatment. She concluded by saying, "It's not hard opening up communication. However, once you've opened it, you're almost in a sense cheating them." She added that she could refer students to the school psychologist who is in the school two days a week for a school of 5,000 kids. However, that would not be very helpful. Where do you go from there, once they have opened up and you have communicated, she asked.

Professor Weiss replied by asking the speaker what she thought she could do and she replied that it was not fair to turn the question back to her. Weiss answered, "If I say to you, 'what do you mean you don't see any place to go with these children?' then you have a right to feel very, very annoyed with me. But a child presents a problem to you and you do feel somewhat hopeless about it. That's information, and really, this is the process of communication we're talking about. The communication is not only between you and the people that you're going to be working with, the communication is between you and you, too. If this is telling you something, then maybe you can make use of what it's telling you." He added he would like to see teachers trained to see things that way. He asked, "What do you do with a feeling of hopelessness when a problem is presented to you. How do you handle it?" He said he thought one has to live through something with one's students. "To what extent are you curious and interested, to what extent are you willing to deal with your own feelings of hopelessness and frustration? How do you deal with them? These kids are very astute, right? You know that, and they pick up things from you that you don't say to them; yet, that you do and that you live with them. Things like emotion. That's not supposed to be part of any curriculum; nobody teaches emotion." The coordinator went on to point out that personal resources, like ego strength, are necessary to handle emotions and that neither emotions nor how to handle them are part of a high school curriculum. He continued to say that personal resources develop out of some kind of action that takes place between people. "Sometimes it doesn't develop very strongly. Sometimes it develops very strongly. Maybe less in some people than in others," he said. He indicated that how one deals with persons with differing ego strengths is another issue of communication. "How you use your resources and how you see the resources of others become really crucial processes in the whole area of communication," he said.

Another speaker responded. He said the school in society has become the repository for curing the social ills of the society. The burdens placed upon the teacher are so monumental because so much has been left there, as to stagger the imagination of any person with goodwill, knowledge, understanding and insight. In a general way, perhaps psychology is an attempt to try to get at those kind of social ills that we see destroying us and others. However, that speaker felt that this conception may be overly difficult and taxing for the teacher. He put it, "It's as if we, the teachers, will be the angels of society, solving the problems that society has helped to create. Perhaps these problems have nothing to do with the educator, per se, or should not be the problems of the educator per se."

Another speaker suggested that the meeting return to

the topic, how to communicate with high school students. Another participant suggested that communication with high school students perhaps was not the topic. He said that what everybody is trying to do is to communicate with themselves. Correspondingly, he felt it was paradoxical to discuss "the problems of the high school kids and there's not one high school kid here." He challenged ideas discussed without such realities. He offered a positive note; "We are a group of people and maybe we are trying to communicate with ourselves."

A woman in the audience took issue with this point of view. She said that teachers deal with students every day and certainly should have some understanding of their problems, whether the high school student is sitting in confrontation or not. Tolstoy wrote about a woman without being a woman. Thus, the discussion of communication seemed to begin with an investigation into the process of the panel, what its purposes were, and how they might be labeled. Communication was the issue: communication with students, communication within the teacher and communication by the teachers in the workshop. A different approach was suggested by a teacher who said he was desperately trying to find better ways to communicate with his students. He said he was one of many social studies teachers teaching psychology, and that he had a good chance to do some basic thinking about the approach to the psychology course. He thought it should be different from most of the usual courses which are taught as standup lectures or lectures disguised as discussions. He was very concerned to know what his students were looking for. He had told his students that he needed to know what they wanted to know. Then he pieced together from their information some idea of the course. His course turned out to be a behavioral one rather than one of the

several other types that can be built. He said he got away
from the front of the room, and got "down with" the
students. His purpose was to communicate with them on
an individual basis. He and the students set up independent
study which occupies about half of the time in this course.
The other half is devoted to somewhat more or less regular
course treatment of basics. While doing independent study,
students choose their topics with the teacher's guidance
and then pursue the topic either on their own initiative or
with his guidance. Because of the time during the week
devoted to independent study, the teacher has a chance to
sit down and talk with the students individually. They
discuss the study that they're working on, baseball, or
anything under the sun, and they eventually get around to
something about psychology. He said he did not know
how this program would turn out, but that he believes this
structure gives him basic communication with students. A
young lady questioned him about the times when the
students might present an explosive personal issue. The
teacher emphasized that he certainly would not take it to
another person, but rather would treat it with confident-
iality and would suggest that the student has other
alternatives. He thought that his overall approach brought
him close to students; however, he continues to search for
better ways.

Another participant said he was going to relate a little
bit of his situation, which was very similar to that of the
previous speaker. He would tell us what he has done in
nine high school psychology courses. This teacher reported
that the most important thing was to come down form the
ivory tower. One of the ways that he tries to communicate
is to find almost any way possible to establish rapport with
the individual student. He has about 25 students as a
maximum for groups. He usually seats the class in a circle

or any variation of the circle the teacher or student might want to use in order to promote rapport and to facilitate ease of operation. He makes about 10 or 12 field trips to mental institutions and institutions for the retarded. He uses many films. The teacher invites five or six speakers from the field of psychology. This teacher emphasized that he was neither a psychologist nor a psychiatrist. He does not attempt nor should high school teachers attempt to handle any case in a clinical manner. He was asked, what to do when the teacher has established rapport with youngsters and a situation develops which warrants help, or guidance. The issues might involve personality difficulties or personal desires or hostilities. What does the teacher do?

This question was answered as follows, "We are not psychologists and all we really can do is listen. They don't want you to solve their problems; they know you can't. All they want you to do is listen."[1]

The question was then raised, would the teacher refer a student to a school counselor or psychologist if these persons were available? The teacher holding forth apparently had had negative experiences. He saw the school psychologist or counselor as people there "in name only." Possibly if we had people *in actuality* plus title, students could be referred, but only with the full knowledge of the student, he commented. The problem of referral was then discussed by a guidance counselor who offered the illustration of one of his students. The student had constantly spoken about suicide. He felt his task to be one of establishing trust in order to refer the boy properly. He spent five months building up a relationship with this kid

---

[1] *Editor's note:* The objection may be raised, of course, that listening is a psychotherapeutic decision and may powerfully serve to open up further issues which are explosive.

and finally, when enough trust was apparent, he sent him to a hospital where he would get proper care. The guidance counselor suggested that a proper question would be not whether referrals should be made, but rather to what sources. He asked, "Are you asking for a list of good qualified agencies who are going to help these kids?

A woman skeptically interjected, "No, we'd have a two-year wait," but was told by the guidance counselor that the boy he referred went down on a Wednesday and made an appointment and saw a psychiatrist on Friday of the same week. Another participant affirmed that one can get the same day service with certain agencies and services.

Another person said that the main point is clear: teachers should not do therapy themselves. The general sentiment was expressed that on the high school level where a teacher may have had only 9 credits in psychology, he's not qualified to do therapy. He can build trust and he can listen and perhaps recommend his students to various agencies that are qualified to help.

Listening to students and communicating with them is perhaps a process that psychology courses can facilitate. Should this facilitation begin early in high school? This new topic was discussed in terms of the general place of psychology in the high school curriculum. In New York City, psychology is introduced as an elective in the social studies curriculum and social studies requires 3½ years. Psychology is then typically offered in the senior year. It was suggested that psychology does not have to be in the social studies curriculum. Perhaps the person teaching it is more important than the department that the person comes out of. Perhaps psychology can be introduced earlier than the senior year. This would depend upon the administration of the school being flexible enough to allow the student to take it.

It was suggested that a recommendation come out of this session, that psychology courses should be introduced as early as possible in the student's curriculum.

Professor Weiss then raised another issue in terms of the communication process. He asked, "To what extent do you think that it is important that you be acquainted with who you are in order to communicate with young people in your classes?"

One person replied to this. She indicated that persons who teach, teach for many reasons. Some teachers not only are not in touch with themselves, but also actively fight any attempt to bring them into touch with themselves. They become defensive. The speaker complained that, "You want to start an in-service workshop in a school to talk about that kind of thing and the immediate reaction from a certain percentage of your faculty is 'Why me?' The in-service workshops that you do manage to start get the people who are in touch with themselves and who really don't need this at all." Her feeling was that to be able to listen and hear students, one must be in touch with oneself. The speaker furthered her challenge concerning the self-knowledge approach to communication. She opined, "If you walk down the halls of any high school, you can tell who your people are by watching the kids in relation to those people. The people at whom the kids smile. The people with whom the kids will stop for a moment's chat between classes are the people who are listening, who are hearing, who are responding. They're the people who can say to a kid, "Look, I don't know what you can do about a situation, but let's go and find out." The speaker felt that there were "people who are not in touch with themselves in this very room this afternoon. How can we get them in touch with themselves? We had people who weren't listening to anybody. Everybody was riding his own little high horse and people were not listening to the other person. How do we get these people to accept the idea of getting into touch with themselves?"

Should it be mandatory to screen very carefully the applicants who teach psychology courses? The idea was put forth that a series of in-service courses could be generated in which teacher self-awareness might occur. Careful curriculum planning would be necessary in order to create such courses. At least one member of the school staff would have to have the training and insight and the capacity to plan such a curriculum.

A student present reported his reaction that "It's not only the students you have to deal with, it's also yourselves, because if you don't want to deal with that, you're always going to have problems teaching. You have to teach a student history, social science, or whatever is taught in school but at the same time you don't always have to put yourself in the place of a teacher." He said he could remember being in school and the teacher saying, "I'm putting this up on the blackboard. If you don't know this, it is your problem." His feeling seemed to be that it is very necessary for students to feel cared about. He suggested that probably there really would be a lot of things one needed to learn about how to relate to children. He ruminated that, "If you finish a class ahead of time, say teaching history or something, why not say to them, 'Let's rap about what you have on your mind.' You'll be surprised what kids have on their minds."

A teacher echoed this student's plea for a humanistic approach. The teacher talked about the Jewish expression "to be a mensch," (to be a person). He said he found this to be the most important thing in effecting communication in teaching. This teacher reported his own experience of surprise that his students became very upset when he had been absent. Perhaps this was because of his attempts to see and talk with students before and after class. Sometimes he has felt over-whelmed by their problems. He told of a 16-to-17 -year-old girl who had said to him just before Christmas, "You know, I hope I get hit by a car before the holiday starts because I don't want to stay home; I'm depressed." He decided to talk to her. He did not want to submit her name for referral unless she was willing. The girl said, "Look, I've been to shrinks, to psychologists. I've had it. I'm full of it." What can be done? The teacher felt that he could act merely as a sounding board for her, and he found this very frustrating.

Another participant took the view that there was communication between the teacher and the girl. Perhaps there were some attitudes or characteristics of the teacher that were effective in the transaction with the student. After all, the student did come to school, and she did talk with this teacher. The participant felt that "rapping" and relating with students was extremely important. She said that, "Kids do have to have something to look forward to. And history and math is not going to make it." She said she knew that from her own experience. She remembered very vividly all of the teachers that she had that meant anything to her. She said that they were all teachers that sat down and "rapped" with students about things that they felt. She concluded that "If you can't relate to a child, you're not going to teach him much (history). You have to make a child want to learn. The only way to do that is to learn about them."

Another woman, a psychologist's assistant in a school, reported dealing with kindergarten, first and second grade kids. She offered, "If you don't think these kids have problems at that age, five or six years old, you're wrong. It's the first time they come out of the home and go into a school system, this is when it all begins. They need someone to listen to them, even at that age."

The participants seemed aware that they were talking about themselves, and that it was necessary to relate their ideas about the communication experienced in the workshop with the communication process in the classroom. A participant stated that it was necessary to develop respect for each other's ideas in the communication process. He said, "We should give a great deal of respect to some of these important questions we raise with ourselves." He also suggested that as far as students in the classrooms are concerned, that when they raise questions or ideas, they be afforded the same atmosphere of respect.

It was his view that something goes on in the group situation that can be made the focus of a good deal of both emotional and intellectual learning.

Another person pointed to the type of experiences in which students can share problems and realize that their own problems are not unique. Students can feel better after such experiences, because "someone else" has a problem equal to their own, or similar to or even more serious than the one they themselves face. This was described as communication and as a very therapeutic kind of learning.

Another participant observed that the previous speaker had, to begin with, certain values and objectives. He went on to reason that if it's important to a teacher that young people be able to share their ideals and feelings with each other, then the teacher would attempt to do something about enhancing that sharing. However, if the value of sharing does not matter to the teacher, there may be other values which displace communication. "Suppose what matters only is that they (students) have absorbed a certain amount of knowledge and can repeat it under certain conditions?" he asked. The teacher can undertake procedures to insure that students attain these goals. The general point would refer again to the teacher's self-knowledge. This includes becoming acquainted with what one's own values and objectives are and being honest about it. The speaker said that knowledge of emphasis allows the teacher to work for effectiveness. If one emphasizes the acquisition of certain fields of knowledge, one should learn to do it well and imaginatively so that students find it a stimulating and thought provoking experience. Thus, self-knowledge might help the teacher increase effectiveness of communication in many ways: Not only by using quasi-therapy (sharing self-knowledge, accepting the students' search for self-knowledge), but also by helping the teacher to clarify his own goals and objectives.

An earlier speaker responded that there was nothing that she had said that indicated that what we should have engaged in is therapy sessions. She observed that the interaction is itself the most profound therapeutic experience that a teacher can offer any child in school; thus, the question of just to be able to communicate is not important. This speaker suggested that by forcing polarity between the rap sessions and the academic psychological curriculum, one forces an unnecessary dichotomy. She reasoned and hoped that if the academic and rap are integrated and done well, psychology would be made alive, dynamic, and meaningful. She said that the high school course does not have to be a rap session or therapy session, but should serve to liberate students to feel, to think and to learn.

These considerations concerning the interactional aspects of communication were subsequently conceptualized and discussed in several ways: one teacher saw interaction as effective when there is mutual reinforcement. A second person offered an existential interpretation, that is, communication would be most effective when the foolishness and absurdity of students' actions would be matched by the teacher's realization of his own foolishness and trends toward it. A third view was that honesty in the interaction could be openly expressed if individual targets are avoided. The variety of conceptualizations seemed balanced by the similarity of concerns: Is communication therapy? Is it group process? What are the constraining forces? What can be done about the teacher's self-knowledge and the attitudes of administrators? How do you synthesize the content and process of the high school psychology experience?

The topics under discussion were debated vigorously. Caution was expressed about the therapeutic role of the secondary school teacher of psychology. It was emphasized that he was not a therapist but, because of his special discipline, he must be very sensitive to his students. While no unanimous conclusion was reached, there was general agreement that in order to communicate effectively with the students, we must be honest with ourselves and honest with them.

11. Communication with High School Students

MARGARET MILLER

I feel a little uncomfortable with a big, wide word like communication. Especially when it has taken on all sorts of nuances of late, ranging from the touching-feeling connotations it has picked up from the sensitivity group movement to the public bemoaning of a lack of it between generations, between student and teacher, among students, and so on ad infinitum. If you strip away all the new accretions of the word and go back to Webster, you find that it once had a fairly simple meaning: "1. act or fact of imparting, bestowing or conveying. 2. intercourse by words, letters or messages; interchange of thoughts or opinions, by conference or other means."

Now the word begins to take on manageable proportions. When we apply it to the high school psychology class, it becomes still more precise, and we can even convert it into an operational definition, defining it in terms of how to do it, or the behaviors which are necessary in our students and ourselves for us to call it communication.

Some of the behaviors we want in our students, indeed must have, if we are to communicate, come quickly to mind: 1. they must come to class (regularly) (and on

This was an invited paper submitted to the Symposium on Problems in High School Psychology, City College of the City University, New York, January 1972.

time!); 2. they must be involved in what is going on in class; 3. outside of class they must read about psychology, do their homework assignments, and begin to observe things psychologically.

Every teacher would agree that these behaviors are absolutely necessary if there is to be any communicating; any bestowing, any interchange of thoughts and opinions. And the converse is true, as well: if all of these behaviors are present, then surely so is communication.

The problem is how to achieve this. Every teacher of students in the last two years of high school knows it is a formidable task. There are so many impinging stimuli: not only the normal problems of development, the agonies of adolescence, the identity crisis, but also the panic generated by the college admissions "mess" and the job and career crisis. I know I've tried — and often failed miserably with many methods, sometimes from taking Holt et. al. too literally, other times from overestimating high school students' ability to "motivate themselves", others from underestimating their ability to understand complex ideas.

Certainly if there's any high school subject in which students could become enthralled and swept up in a fervor of studying — just for the joy of knowing — it should be psychology. It's certainly relevant, immediate, meaningful. It's what high school students say they care about most: themselves and other people, why they are like they are, and do what they do. However, that simply isn't enough. They *are* fascinated by psychology, but the long range goal of reading that article or book or planning that experiment simply isn't a strong enough reinforcement to compete with the coke now at the corner coffee shop, or the long telephone conversation tonight about the cute new boy or last Saturday's soccer game. Somebody else will read the article, and then you can fake it.

That's the key word, I think: reinforcement. Behavior is a function of its consequences. Behavior which is reinforced will increase in frequency. The magnitude of the reinforcement determines the strength and persistence of the response. So to get the behavior you want in class (and out) — to increase the opportunity for communication — you first have to specify the behavior you want, then identify the reinforcers. The psychology class must have stronger reinforcers than most competing stimuli.

What are some things that are reinforcing for high school students in a class? I can think of three: 1. knowing they're doing something important, that matters, 2. knowing they're doing it well, and 3. getting recognition for it.

Of course psychology is important; we all acknowledge that. It's important to understand yourself and others. But what I mean is that it should be presented as a serious discipline, on an adult level, not as a watered-down, oversimplified approach. Kids know when they're being treated with condescension. They love to use the vocabulary, and they can grasp the concepts if they're given the chance. I think its importance is best seen when it is taught as a science, and constantly related to "life". You don't leave the fun out. Ideas are often best understood through role playing, experiments, and other active means. We play games and we have contests, like one where the students bring in examples of operent behavior they observe on the bus, in a classs, or at home. They vote for the best one, and the prize is, of course, a bag of M & M's. We talk about what psychologists do and more important, we *do* what psychologists do. We run serious experiments, we analyze, we record, we evaluate, we test. We go to lectures by real psychologists at a nearby university.

The students are learning a lot, and they know it from two sources. I let them know by my comments, by showing my delight at their ideas and accomplishments. I reinforce behavior I want, and also their successive approximations. And they keep running records to see for themselves. They take many short quizzes. The quizzes are given randomly and they are cumulative. The first assures that they read the assignments and take notes; the second shows them their mastery (and keeps them reviewing their notes). If they have a valid reason for missing a quiz, they can take another form of it later. Tests thus begin to lose their punitive meaning and take on a new significance for self-evaluation. Tests are no longer so threatening because there are so many that no single one is fatal. There's no reason to give up toward the end of the term because you're so far behind.

After each quiz, some time is taken to reteach whatever anybody didn't understand. One result of this is that I haven't been able to cover as much material as I wished. (I still have twinges of guilt about that and have to keep reminding myself that it's attitudes and methods I want to establish — they'll forget all the facts anyway.) What I have covered, everybody really understands. They know a dependent variable from an independent variable, and they know the difference between positive punishment and negative reinforcement for example; and they love being told that I know many a college student who's confused about those terms. There's a growing feeling of confidence in that class, and also a growing skepticism and criticism which is really exciting!

The students must have a variety of ways in which to succeed. If they have trouble with the tests at first (when they get so many, they do start mastering them), they can do well in laboratory work. At least two periods per week are devoted to experiments. We do them with the class as a whole, or divided into smaller groups. In the second term when we go into some of the usual topics of an introductory course — perception, personality, groups, etc. — pairs of students go through folders filled with experiments I've collected and plan and conduct the ones they've chosen. Thus everyone has a chance to run the class and get feedback that way. During the year each student must design and carry out an experiment of his own, and then present it to the class at the end of the year. They can select something they're really interested in and enjoy the heady feeling of doing something original and on their own. This often gives them the confidence to participate in other aspects of the class.

The behavior of being involved in discussion can be increased by really listening to what each student says, acknowledging what was said, never "putting it down." Every contribution has some validity, and sometimes you can miss the grain of wisdom if you don't really listen to it and perhaps ask for further explanation. Sometimes you can effectively silence a student for the rest of the year by not giving a response total respect. While reinforcement requires time to establish behavior, avoidance can easily be established by just one incident of punishment.

The most important form of recognition for a high school student is grades. Rightly or wrongly, they've been conditioned by now into regarding that form of reinforcement as the highest glory. I don't grade on the curve; I announce in the beginning of the course what the criterion for an "A" is, and add that there's no reason why everyone in the class can't earn one. Lots of little reinforcements seem to be more effective than one massive one, especially when the large one is in the distant future, so the little quizzes become very important. The students keep a running record of their total points.

The use of a programmed textbook, such as the one used in my course, can lead to boredom. To combat this the students are given sheets of paper with lots of little boxes to be filled in as they go along in the book, and the sheets have to be turned in for credit. Points are given for lots of things, and any student who gets 90 percent of the total possible points at the end of the term doesn't have to take the exam. (But only one out of three who qualified this year opted out of the midyear exam).

When you start looking at a class in terms of behaviors and reinforcers, you can begin to control the behaviors. A cold-blooded approach, some would say. Not at all, when the results are that everybody in the class being happy with each other, and studying and communicating like mad! And you don't have to be sneaky about it either; you can openly discuss the reinforcers present in the class, and this too encourages the students to look at behavior that way. In my class this year, the students come to class and even bring notebooks and pens. They are increasingly arriving on time, or sending messages when they can't. Some who were excused from one class because of a conflict with an art class have made other arrangements and come to psychology. They are lively and totally involved in discussion, pouncing gleefully on any weak point in an argument, or flaw in an experiment, demanding operational definitions of each other. This doesn't happen all at once, and there are plenty of plateaus in the curve. Therefore you have to think about reinforcing yourself, and even keep records of the incidence of the behaviors you are concerned with, or discouragement will set in from time to time.

But gradually it does happen, the behavior is shaped, and then you have communication.

12. Communicating With Adolescent Students: An Experiential Approach

ALFRED WEISS

I was very much taken with what Professor Brown was discussing—particularly with respect to Professor Sprinthall's new approach in combining academic learning with student experience. While I was in Amsterdam this summer, I noticed across the canal a little wine cellar called *Le Bon Marriage* (the good marriage). In this case, the good marriage was between wine and cheese and indeed, there was a delightful blending of ingredients. During the past five years, I have observed the increased possiblity of academic learning (through lecture, reading, and other traditional modes) and individual experience evolving into a "good marriage". From my own experience, the procedure of working with individual experience first, and then connecting it to some broad generalized principle or to a theoretical issue, academic in nature, seems one of the happiest kinds of marriage. However, there are certainly times when the marriage seems strained. Individual student experiences do not always lend themselves easily to organizing principles. It is hardly ever possible to "arrange" for life experiences pertinent to

This paper was presented at the Seminar on the Teaching of High School Psychology, New York, City College, September 1971.

course subject matter to evolve from settings outside the classroom; however, one can attempt to have such experiences emerge within the classroom wherever possible. This notion is based on the premise that while human experiences are uniquely different, they are at the same time, very similar. Clearly, the teacher must be original and careful in his planning for shared experiences around issues. Although this is vital, it need not inhibit your following what appear to be meaningful detours.

If I planned to introduce Erikson's stages of development to my college class, I would walk into the room, sit at the back, and wait for the groups to initiate a discussion. Usually there would be an initial silence, followed by expressed annoyance or resentment and questions like, What is going on? After engaging in some discussion concerning their feelings of anger, frustration and confusion, the class and I would examine Erikson's presentation of *initiative* as a stage of development following that of autonomy. The relevance of earlier experiences in regard to current behavior becomes more clear in light of the students' shared classroom experience. Frequently, I might add, students note that school experiences have rarely encouraged a sense of initiative. This learning experience differs qualitatively from one in which I might lecture on the "stages of development" as posited by Erikson.

Only recently, in an exchange of experiences regarding pets (which I had expected to relate to projected feelings and growth of psychological defense in childhood), the class appeared concerned with the effects of breeding. This concern led to questions of genetic versus environmental influences. It is clear that the students' classroom experiences may have very unique connotations, not only in terms of their academic learning but also in terms of their personal living. This merger, between the intellectual and the affective has resulted in a special kind of learning. My study of this indicates that college students stimulate their own thinking processes actively under these conditions. The experiential approach would appear to be highly appropriate for a high school adolescent population. By making use of shared experiences, planned and unplanned, we can create a more meaningful learning atmosphere.

What is the relevance of a course in psychology to the high school curriculum, to the students' development, and to his ability to draw meaning from the school experience? First, I would like to refer to a question raised in a previous talk; namely, does a course in pre-college psychology make sense *only* for a select group of students. Perhaps, it makes as much sense to teach psychology as a required subject to all students as it does to teach American history for the fourth, fifth or sixth time in high school students' school lives. In my view, the study of psychology as a means of dealing with perspectives in their own lives (in addition to preparing them for a possible career in teaching, social work, clinical psychology, etc., or to simply "learning about" psychological materials) makes preeminently good sense for adolescents.

Why is this so? The high school students are at a unique and difficult point of development. They are adolescents; of course the meaning of adolescence does seem to change from generation to generation. However, you, as teacher, are going to have an opportunity of dealing with students who at this time in our history, have been confronting some very major difficulties in terms of every day living. (See, for example, Kenniston, 1960; Friedenberg, 1959.) Such difficulties abound; we might only consider parent-adolescent relationships; or deal with adolescent aspects of peer relationship. Or we could explore the influence of cultural factors and the special interests, energies or fashions adolescent age groups tend to display. Shall we deal with the entire disaffection with the "establishment", and the wish to replace it with a form as yet unformed in the students' minds? Perhaps the special qualities of cognition with tremendous sources of energy peculiar to this age might be explored (see Bruner, 1971), or the unique physical development inherent in this period and its consequences in experience might be further understood. Certainly any one of these points of difficulty in development would be enough in itself to warrant an attempt at psychological education. Moreover, each of these particular areas, can be associated with some very thoughful work that has been done by a number of psychologists in the field, not only in terms of adolescents per se, but also in terms of general psychological principles. Lastly, I believe that through the examination of the students' shared experiences we may discover the rich potential of working with a high school population.

Before continuing the discussion of the experiential approach some possible reference sources for your consideration are in order:

1. *Freedom to Learn,* a book by Carl Rogers (1969), discusses a humanistic approach to relationships. Rogers prefers the term "facilitator" to "teacher," since it implies for him greater respect for intrinsic motivation. This has profound consequences for the growing independence in the adolescent population. You should find it a stimulating presentation of alternative perceptions of learning.

2. A book written by Leeper and Madison (1959), who are Gestaltists at heart, entitled *Toward Understanding Human Personalities,* which I recommend to you as a very

reasonable approach to development, with a good deal of solid research to supplement issues of the growth of personality. This book contains relevant case studies of behavior at different ages.

3. Jerome Bruner has already been mentioned as a fine source in dealing with the cognitive approach in the classroom. Recently in the *Relevance of Education (1971)* (a series of essays) while discussing issues involved in such acquisition of knowledge, Bruner began to deal with the influences of intentionality, social class and poverty on learning.

4. Richard Jones (1968), in *Fantasy and Feeling in Education* comments on Bruner's cognitive emphasis and presents his own case for some kind of marriage between affective states and moral-academic learning requirements. His chapter titled "Toward a Complete Theory of Instruction" should be read especially by those who are concerned about having to become therapists in the classroom.

5. Heath (1972) in an article in the *University of Chicago School Review* presents a potent argument for the integration of the feelings and values of young people with their intellectual development.

There is need for alerting teachers to the richness inherent in their attending to human behavior as expressed by their students on several levels — not solely the cognitive level. Attempting to merge levels of awareness may be risky in that such exchanges may prove barren as well as highly fruitful. However, I feel that it's worth the risk because something develops out of this sense of perspective; out of the student's own life. I do not think this kind of learning is replaceable by simply telling students how to live their lives, or having them only read about how they should lead their lives. In other words, they arc thinking, feeling and functioning in the classroom in certain ways, and the delineation of these realities makes for experiences which I have not found duplicated in other contexts.

In a somewhat similar vein I can't really describe today's adolescents; I can experience it with you, perhaps, but I can't describe it to you so that you understand it fully or completely. Maybe *some* of it comes through in what I've been saying. You have lives of your own which you can share with the students you teach. They learn about you as much as you get to learn about them. They read you! They react to you in ways which they feel can meet certain predictions that they make about your behavior, while you're concentrating on how they're going to react to what you're doing. Is that an important piece of information for you? I suppose that it only becomes important in terms of how it is used—hopefully, it could lead to honest teacher and student interchanges, to reflection and to a sense of self-worth. Adolescents are going through a very trying period of their lives. If you share with them not only your competent knowledge but a bit of your own unique experiences, you permit them to place in perspective their own lives vis a vis what is going on around them. Let us take just one example. If in the course of your relationship with the students in the psychology course you enable them to take a look at their parents in ways which are slightly different from ways in which they are accustomed to looking at them, you will have done an incomparable service.

As far as an overall approach to teaching adolescents in a pre-college psychology course is concerned, I'll conclude with this thought. I have found it very important that teachers respect their own adolescent experiences—a difficult order sometimes. I'm not saying that you have to love these experiences or feel that they were very wonderful because they weren't all very wonderful. They were just as trying for you in many respects as they are for the present adolescent generation. However, I do think you must respect those experiences as part of your own development and that you must make use of them. I think you must find ways of sharing their significance with your adolescent students, in order to really engage the richness of their experience. I'll go further: where you think your adolescent life was completely barren and deniable, you're going to find it extremely difficult to teach adolescents. I invite you, at this time, to raise questions of your own and feel free to address those questions to any of the speakers.

REFERENCES

Bruner, J. S. *The relevance of education*. New York: W. W. Norton, 1971.

Friedenberg, E. Z. *The vanishing adolescent,* Boston: Beacon Press, 1959.

Heath, D. H. Affective education: Aesthetics and Discipline. *University of Chicago School Review,* May 7, 1972.

Jones, R. M. *Fantasy and feeling in education.* New York: New York University Press, 1968.

Keniston, K. *The uncommitted.* New York: Dell, 1960.

Leeper, R. Q. & Madison, P. *Toward understanding human personalities.* New York: Appeleton, 1959.

Maslow, A. *Motivation and personality.* New York: Harper & Row, 1954.

Rogers, C. R. *Freedom to learn.* Columbus, Ohio: Charles E. Merrill, 1969.

ADDITIONAL REFERENCES

Borton, T. *Reach, touch and teach: Student concerns and process education.* New York; McGraw-Hill, 1970

Goethas, G. W. & Klos, D. S. *Experiencing youth: First persons accounts.* Boston: Little, Brown & Co., 1970

Holt, J. *How children fail.* New York: Pitman, 1964

Jersild, A. T. *In search of self.* New York: Columbia University Press, 1952

Weinstein, G., & Fan Fantini, M.D. (Eds.) *Toward humanistic education: A curriculum of affect.* New York: Praeger, 1970

13. Editor's Analysis of Communication with the Adolescent Student

Perhaps it is most important to ask not *how* to best communicate, and not even *what* to communicate, but rather to ask *why* communicate with your students. What are your goals in a high school course in psychology? This is an extraordinarily difficult question. If your goals are to teach specific content or even to teach about what psychologists do and who they are, you can assume either Alfred Weiss' *or* Margaret Miller's approach. Weiss' view is that content must be experienced to be meaningful; experience is action, indeed interaction, between the teacher and student. Miller's view is that content has to be reinforced; the student has to be present in class and the teacher's evidence of respect has to be made manifest. Well, obviously reinforcement can be many things: an act of listening, an act of approving, or even an act of rewarding a student with a grade or an "M & M." A student behavior and a teacher reinforcement is just as much an experiential intersect as is a feeling of empathy that results from a student action and a teacher understanding (another form of reinforcement).

Can it be that both the experiential and the reinforcement views are the same? Or that they are both correct? Can it be that communication is a false issue and that specific curricular goals are the only issues?

187

If the experiential and reinforcement views are one and the same, how is it that so much heat and light is generated about "getting close to students," "coming away from the ivory tower" on one hand, and "giving the students solid information," assuring their performance on "specified objectives" by "consistent reinforcement" on the other?

Apparently at some level "experience" can be translated into action, reaction, reinforcement and interaction. Apparently also, these latter concepts can be conceived in such a way that they "include" experiences. Some teachers prefer one set of concepts in their language about what happens in the classroom, and some other teachers prefer what often seems a different language. The experiential teacher is obviously concerned with the quality of the interaction and perhaps even enjoys being involved in social intersects. The reinforcement approach is one in which the teacher steps away from the intersect long enough to label the teacher's actions and the students' actions.

We have described teachers speaking two different languages and perhaps playing two different social roles *vis-a-vis* the students. Apparently there are three steps necessary before we can say that these teachers are communicating *with each other:*

1. The first step is to begin talking. This brings out the different teacher languages and different perceptions of social role.
2. The second step is to find the similarities in language and in social (teaching) role. This step in communication is certainly like concept formation.
3. The third step is to formulate agreed upon goals.

Of course a fourth step would involve implementation and evaluation of whether or not goals are being met.

It is interesting that these steps seem easier to identify and follow when we consider curriculum by itself. However, as Miller and Weiss both point out, this may not really be possible.

In the workshop and in the papers presented in this chapter we proceed through step one, and partially through step two. At this point a careful study of the underlying goals of the classroom teacher requires great flexibility with the psychological lexicon and language. In other words, the teacher really has to know a good deal about psychology himself to now create a language which shows the similarities between himself and his colleagues with respect to their perception of meaningful teaching, meaningful learning and meaningful curriculum.

I guess this editor does believe at this juncture that the "heat and light" represents two things: one, a healthy attempt by the teachers of high school psychology to communicate with each other and with their students, and two, a need for more psychological knowledge and flexibility with concepts of motivation, concept formation, social interaction and the like. In this connection I am suggesting, along with my previously stated views concerning the training of the secondary school teacher of psychology, that, in general, such teachers interact and communicate much more with psychologists and educational psychologists. Goal setting is a matter of knowing what you want, what others want, what it means to "want," and perhaps even what one ought to want.

Part 3: Teacher Training

14. Workshop on Teacher Training

HARWOOD FISHER, Coordinator
ETHEL WEISS, Editor

The purpose of this chapter is to provide a summary and analysis of the teacher training discussion which was held at the Symposium on Problems in High School Psychology.[1] The workshop included several teachers of high school psychology and also teacher trainers. The discussion was chaired by Professor Fisher. The objectives were to raise and identify two sets of issues. The first was that of teacher training in general, and the second, the needs of the psychology teacher, in particular.

It is somewhat illuminating to note that the social studies background of most of the psychology teachers who were present dominated their concerns in several ways.

There seems to be a struggle to integrate the social studies concepts with those of psychology. This attempt to bridge the gap is not only a concern over content, but also a struggle over how to teach. The social studies teacher, especially in New York City, seems to come under attack by students for "irrelevant" content. Those teachers who enter a new door to teach psychology, as an alternative

[1]Symposium on Problems in High School Psychology; Workshop entitled Problems in course curricula, City College of the City University, New York, 1972.

course, are evidently concerned with this problem. Hence, on one hand, they strive for contact with students and for a focus on process and dynamics. On the other hand, they seem to yearn for a content approach for two reasons: (1) to reduce dissonance with their own background as trained teachers, and (2) because they do not have the content mastery in psychology.

In view of these considerations, it is understandable that the workshop discussion began by pursuing general issues in teacher-training which affect all secondary school teachers and, indeed, which affect secondary school curriculum. The social studies teacher and his teacher-training counterparts began to see changes in their roles and in the courses they offer. The questions at the outset of the workshop reflected these concerns.

The first speaker identified himself as a secondary school teacher of history, who also has taught on the college level. His role as teacher trainer included work with 116 student teachers. He opened two problems for consideration:

1. Are we sacrificing effective teaching of mandated courses in order to offer more and more elective courses?

2. How do we remediate the problem of teachers who are "woefully unequipped" in terms of practical field experiences and specifically in terms of the teaching of high school psychology?

The first speaker reported that he found very many of his student teachers undertrained not only in the disciplines of history, economics and social studies, but also in the psychology of the students that they were to teach. He pointed out that in the New York City system a student is allowed to select an elective in his twelfth year, and that more and more schools are selecting psychology courses as electives.[1] Under these circumstances one can certainly echo the speaker's concern about the teacher's lack of knowledge of content. The speaker seemed to connect the issues of lack of preparation in general with the problem of the preparation of the teacher of psychology. He indicated that, "Psychology is only a twelfth-year elective. Every youngster in the New York City school system must take a year of geography, a year of world history, a year of American studies, and six months of economics, as the mandated course, as long as we maintain the diploma rule." Therefore certainly one could argue that "if we can't get qualified teachers to teach mandated areas, it is frivolous to discuss special training for teachers of psychology." This interweaving of issues is as pointed out above, a natural concern of the social studies teacher. As such we cannot dismiss the general training issues as "important but irrelevant" to the high school psychology course. Rather, the questions have to be reformulated to ask, perhaps more realistically, who should be teaching the high school psychology course. This issue emerged by way of the first speaker's pointing to the popularity of psychology as a high school elective, and by way of his raising the general question of what is an effective teacher.

These points were brought together when a second speaker raised the issue of what the specific training of the high school behavioral science teacher should be.

We may formulate the third major issue of the discussion in the form of a question: In light of the popularity of high school psychology courses, do we use unprepared teachers or do we wait until programs have been established to train teachers, and then offer the high school electives?

[1] *Editor's note:* In the fall of 1972 more than twenty New York City High Schools offered or were developing courses in psychology.

The second speaker was the coordinator of fieldwork in the School of Education at City College, New York.

His first point was that if we don't know enough about how to make an effective teacher we certainly ought to focus as best we can on that which we do know, which is specific subject matter. In the case of the high school psychology teacher, we can insure "that a person graduating from any institution know as much as possible about psychology. Then we can deal with the pedagogy, with methods of transmitting this knowledge and information to others." He went on to point out that we should not spend an inordinate amount of time on how to relate if there is nothing to relate. The first suggestion to emerge here, then, is that psychology teachers (de facto or ideal) must be taught psychology.

Secondly the question of remediating the lack of teacher's knowledge may not be answered by a spoon-feeding operation,[2] but rather with a retraining[3] process. The speaker pointed out that, "We have people teaching anthropology, sociology and psychology who were never taught to teach these areas. Should they be retrained? Or are there people available who do know something about anthropology, who do know something about psychology, who do know something about sociology, who perhaps know little about teaching or who have taken minimal education training." He went on to suggest that from his

---

[2] *Editor's note:* One wonders in this connection whether the "quickie" attractive "methods of teaching urban high school psychology" course is not often an unrealistic solution in contrast to the programs described more fully in this book. One wonders in the same connection what the "Summer" institute or in-service "minicourse" can really do relative to problems in retraining.

[3] *Editor's note:* It is the view of this editor that both retraining of de facto teachers and newly conceived training programs (such as Johnson's, Part 5) must be developed simultaneously.

perspective "students ultimately would be better off having these people retrain to transmit this information which they already possess, rather than trying to spoon-feed the information to people who perhaps possess the quality of being able to transmit information to students, or perhaps not, but who are not familiar with the specific content areas."[4]

In terms which are also suggestive for new training programs, it was suggested that "instead of thinking of an undergraduate education major for somebody who's going to teach high school psychology, consider an undergraduate psychology major who then takes a master's degree in teaching high school at the secondary level. On the master's level he can learn as much as he could have on the undergraduate level, while having already attained a good knowledge of psychology." The speaker made a strong point for having a master's level program in the teaching of high school psychology.

There seemed apparent uniformity in this discussion relative to the issue of the need for training. Who is to do the training and how would be appropriate for the varied teachers, de facto, and "yet to be born?" Even if these are answerable questions now, how does one discuss the needs of the high school which demands its psychology courses right away?

In line with the issue of who should train the high school psychology teacher and what kind of program is

[4]*Editor's note:* This editor has experienced many problems in assessing the background of psychologists and nonpsychologists applying for post-master's training in the teaching of high school psychology. The school psychologist who applies for training has the additional problem of not being included in the state's (New York) certification rubric. However, that problem aside, refocus for such candidates should ideally involve educational psychology courses while emphasize classroom research on teaching and learning.

needed, a participant raised a major problem: how do we eliminate the communication gap between the high school teacher of psychology and the college teacher of psychology? This question includes the gap between the high school teacher and the college education professor. This speaker was critical of the competence of the people who teach and supervise student teachers. Such people, it was felt, should spend a definite amount of time in the high schools or should at least have a definite interest in what is happening in the high school. One of the big problems the speaker found in her own experience student teaching many years ago and also in her talks with current student teachers, is the feeling of lack of communication between the high school teacher and the college teacher trainer. Many professors of education teach the current theories and idealized notions of what should be happening in the high schools rather than responding to what is actually occurring in the high schools. When that person who is student teaching goes into the classroom with the wisdom of his professor's notes, how much real understanding does the student teacher have of the actual classroom situation? The speaker felt strongly that in many cases there is an academic-like feeling "that if you teach at the college level, you're superior." Consequently, the college teacher doesn't have anything to do with the high school teacher. "There's not a willingness in many cases to share ideas, and to communicate between the high school teacher and the teacher trainer in the college." The speaker reasoned that "because of his attitude and his lack of experience, the college teacher cannot provide the student teacher with an adequate background to be able to cope with a real teaching situation."

The question of communication is of course a most serious one, and is dealt with more at length in Part 2. The speaker's remarks are cogent here with respect to two issues: first, the classroom teacher of psychology wants to know, who is going to train him, and exactly what pretensions training programs have; secondly, what role will the "student" play in these programs.

It is necessary to say here that in a training program courses, course offerings and the expertise of the staff ought to be specifically stated, and well thought out. Decisions must be made on the proportions of educational psychology, psychology, general behavioral science, methods and fieldwork to be offered. This certainly does not answer the communication gap; what it does do is to say what is going to be communicated and by whom.

The issue of the role of the student must be carefully built into any training program. How can the student work with the professor in understanding classroom process and the adolescent student; what are the dimensions of this associateship;[5] can student and professor do research and create curriculum together. Some strong independent study component with close faculty associateship and supervision seems in order.

At this point in the workshop, the Coordinator interposed some of his own views. Psychologists in a school of education may be at a particular advantage, in terms of developing a program for high school teacher of psychology. They are in a position from which they cannot pretend they know any more than is known about the issue of how to teach pedagogy. This is healthy for good communication, since it allows the student to more fully

---

[5] *Editor's note:* The secondary school classroom teacher-evaluation of texts, materials, and curriculum offers invaluable concrete detail which can be discussed in terms of psychological and educational principles.

assume his role as a person who is going to have much to discover (if he has yet to teach) and as a person who has much to interchange (if he is already teaching).

Further, psychologists in a school of education are in a position of marrying educational psychology with psychology. They can put together their knowledge about learning and teaching processes with their knowledge of certain specific research areas in psychology, such as learning, development, measurement, motivation and social psychology. Programs which develop to train psychology teachers in the high schools should be programs which involve schools of education and their psychologists, as well as psychology departments. He said that certain courses should be taught by psychologists from outside the school of education. He gave as an example, a course in experimental psychology. He summarized his position as including two points, one is the issue of putting together knowledge of a particular subject area and knowledge of how to teach that subject area. This issue is perhaps one that can be given unique treatment when the educational psychologist trains the teacher of psychology. The second point perhaps reinforces the first: the training of the high school psychology teacher needs to involve a coordinated effort of schools of education and psychology departments in schools of liberal arts.

As was indicated above these considerations of training are foreground against the background of realities: students want high school psychology courses, and administrators and chairmen want them taught.

An acting chairman of a social studies department at a New York City high school, raised a very practical question. He asked whether he should recommend that a psychology course be started at his school now. He stated that he knew that in his department there were no people who were prepared to teach psychology. He wondered whether he should just simply say, "well, since no one is prepared then let it wait a year or two. Let's wait until City College, or Pace College, or Brooklyn College or whoever it is, prepares people through a behavioral science program, and we get people who are licensed, and therefore, qualified." Or, he asked, does he have the obligation to say, "if there is someone who's interested in this perhaps we should encourage him to try his hand at it. Our students aren't being reached by traditional offerings." One of the reasons he stated that he came to the conference was to see if possibly behavioral sciences, could be taught in schools like his, might an introduction to behavioral science interest youngsters in more traditional subjects, he asked.

A high school teacher responded by citing his own experiences at another New York City high school. He stated that in his school students had a choice of selecting their own subjects. "We have four cycles during the year. During cycle two we're offering behavioral science, and close to 300 students chose to take it, and are very happy with it. There is an interest, the students do feel involved. They're getting away from the Social Science approach, because they felt that Social Science was an experience of just going through remembering dates in history, etc. The kids now feel that they are participating in a program. There are laboratory experiences at our school dealing with surveys, polls, public opinion, attitudes of people right now." However, this teacher did question implementing such a program with the right teachers. Teachers in his school made the point that the younger people who are just graduating from college, are going to be the ones who teach these courses. He felt that older people would feel improperly prepared and would be reluctant to teach it.

He stated that one thing that disturbed him was the question of whether the people who are teaching it now, are doing it for the right reasons. For example, he wondered whether they were trying to find themselves. He certainly felt the need to be very cautious about the qualifications of teachers of psychology. He was concerned about "current fads of encounter groups and sensitivity training." He felt that the average teacher who wants to try these techniques in class, is not properly trained, and that such procedures applied by untrained people could have very serious implications. His conclusion was optimistic. He thought that the young people who are graduating with master's and bachelor's degrees in psychology will be the people who will be teaching such courses.

Teachers and administrators do want trained teachers, but they do want to get their courses off the ground. The first speaker offered the opinion that an administrator, if pressed, could have a high school psychology course ready for teaching rapidly. However, he argued that the teacher would really have to be a person with the following in his readiness: empathy, interest, the background, the perception and the knowledge of the student body.

A previous speaker interjected that he was getting the feeling that some people were saying *any* psychology course is better than *no* psychology course. And that, furthermore, if no one was prepared to teach the course, the school could send someone to an institute or seminar in psychology for training. He suggested as an alternative hiring people who were trained in psychology and who are currently unemployed.

It was clear at this juncture that some intermediate steps were necessary to meet the needs of the schools, the teachers and the pupils. The workshop coordinator offered the following as an idea that fell between the training programs needed and the current need for course offerings:

New York State is moving toward the concept of competency-based certification, and that concept can be employed to a certain extent in terms of the issues that have just been raised. Who can become, at the present time, the high school psychology teacher, is separate from the question of who should be the psychology teacher in the future and what sort of undergraduate and graduate programs we should design for the best of all possible times. At present, using the concept of competency-based teaching or competency-based certification, one could train teachers from the point of view of the school, from the point of view of the needs of the community, and from the point of view of the school of education or the training institution. From each of these three points of view, at present, training criteria may be set, which all would agree would represent minimum competency. This does not necessarily end up in state certification or the like. State certification, at least in New York State, is taken care of under the generic rubric of social science. Therefore, the question of who's going to teach the psychology course is partially answered. The question of whether that person is really prepared to teach the psychology course could be an issue which could be resolved by a consortium or a consultation between the community, the school and the teacher-training institution. From the perspective of the teacher-training institution, we think that the person who is now teaching psychology on the pre-college level ought to have mastery of a certain domain of knowledge. As an example of this, our training sequence at City

College sets up a series of prerequisites for specific training in the area of teaching psychology on the high school level. It would not take us too long to go into our own program and say: people teaching now should have such and such prerequisites and should be taking such and such courses to insure their .competency in the area of psychology, over the next period of time, number of months or years. We might certainly learn a good deal if we set up such minimal competencies within the consortium arrangement referred to.

Another participant in the conference said that there were some meetings just beginning in Washington, at the American Psychological Association, on the issue of guidelines for teacher education in psychology. No doubt these guidelines can be very helpful. However, it may even be more helpful for local studies to be made. If the college works in concert with the school and the community, many important issues are bound to surface.

The discussion concluded with a series of considerations relative to setting up new retraining and training programs. This overview evolved from the discussion. In the future, the training for high school psychology teachers should proceed somewhat along the following lines: the high school psychology teacher need not have been an undergraduate psychology major, but at some point he should have a series of core courses within the undergraduate psychology major. Certainly, one does not want to prevent the physics major or the chemistry major or the history major from going into psychology. The master's level training should shift to the behavioral sciences. The person should be trained in anthropology, sociology and psychology. Partly, this is a practical decision based on the anticipation that the high schools are moving in the direction of offering science courses and then perhaps a second course like psychology or anthropology or sociology. It is important that the high school teacher has a broad base in the behavioral sciences. Post-master's preparation would be for 30 credits after the master's degree. (See the sample program display in Chapter 16.) Also in the future, in this connection we need to consider the training of the community college teacher of psychology. That may be a very difficult area, because the community college teacher of psychology does not particularly want to be separated from the senior college teacher of psychology. This separation may not be justifiable. The problems in each type of school are different.

Another future direction is the doctoral program in the teaching of pre-college psychology. That kind of program, most certainly, should be able to include the master's degree in behavioral science.

In the discussion many questions came up concerning the future of teacher-training programs in high school psychology. The discussion concluded on a point of optimism. Recounted was the popularity of the high school psychology course, the curiosity of the high school student, the desire of the teachers to know more about their subject area, and the desire of college educators and other psychologists to be of assistance.[6]

As more and more schools are beginning to offer psychology as an elective on the high school level and as the course becomes increasingly more popular, one has been forced to turn to the questions, What teachers will be teaching these courses?, and How will they be trained?

---

[6]*Editor's note:* Some of the efforts of the American Psychological Association are reviewed in Professor Engle's article in Section I. In addition the Division 2 (Teaching) Panel on Pre-college Teaching offers advisory services to the high school teachers.

This workshop on teacher-training focused upon questions of teaching high school psychology, but at the same time raised important issues regarding the training and preparation of any teacher. Several key issues became evident through the discussion. These can be summarized as follows:

1. Are we sacrificing effective teaching of mandated courses in order to offer more and more elective courses?

2. How do we remediate the problem of teachers being "woefully unequipped" in terms of practical field experiences in general and in the teaching of high school psychology in particular?

3. How do we eliminate the communication gap between the high school teacher of psychology and college teacher of psychology?

4. Because of the popularity of high school psychology courses, do we use unprepared teachers or do we wait until programs have been established to train teacher's and then offer courses in these elective areas?

5. Who are the sources of labor for the teaching of high school psychology: unemployed psychologists, teachers of social studies, health education teachers working within a school?

6. How do we avoid the trap of current fadism and teach lasting concepts and ideas?

7. Do we train teachers to teach content or to teach human relations?

8. How can we establish programs which train teachers effectively in both content areas and pedagogical techniques?

9. At what level of training should the teacher of high school psychology be developed?

The individuals participating in the workshop did not expect to answer these questions specifically, but to raise issues for consideration. A most important point to be brought out in Chapter 14 with regard to training is the idea of applying that which we know about the psychology of learning to the training of psychology teachers. If the psychology teachers do not "practice what they preach" or apply principles of effective learning, how then can other teachers be expected to employ these techniques. (This point will be developed in Chapter 15, Professor Brown's paper.)

15. Preparation in the Psychology of Learning for High School Psychology Teachers

MARION R. BROWN

Recent trends in educational innovation aim to change the school to fit the needs, interests, and abilities of the learner. The learner is encouraged to take the initiative and the responsibility for his own learning. This requires teachers and students who work together in the application of learning psychology to enhance the learner's development. The learner as well as the teacher needs to be aware of how to facilitate his learning. The functions of the teacher of psychology in the secondary school could be considered to include: (1) teaching psychology to students by providing appropriate learning experiences; (2) working as a member of the school community with administrators and other teachers on the provision of interdisciplinary learning experiences and on study of the psychological effects of school structure and general practices; and (3) assisting in evaluation and measurement

This paper was presented at the Symposium on Problems in High School psychology, City College of the City University, New York, January 1972.

of learning in relation to psychological objectives, including the use of feedback from evaluations for future-planning (Shane, 1971). Without these psychological services the present innovations would tend to be associated with the personalities of the innovators and there would be a lack of the systematic study and analysis of innovations necessary to derive basic psychological principles and dynamic research. Preparation for teaching psychology at the secondary level may be demanding, but, undertaken with zeal and imagination, it can be a focal point in the evolution of the educational system and of our society.

What evidence is there to support this statement? The examination of six recent trends in educational innovation provides this evidence. Moreover, analysis of these trends indicates the kind of preparation the teacher of high school psychology would require for the school envisioned for the future.

RECENT TRENDS IN EDUCATIONAL INNOVATION

One trend is the recent literature on education, which has directed attention to the unanticipated, and presumably unintended, psychological consequences of schooling (Coleman, 1966; Friedenberg, 1967; Jackson, 1968; Mosher & Sprinthall, 1969, 1970, 1971). It is observed that teachers are, whether they realize it or not, psychological educators. Children are taught that they are to remain dependent, compliant, and competitive for the outward signs of achievement whether or not learning is meaningful. In this context the demand has come for deliberate, planned teaching of psychology in the schools. The call is for teachers who can help students and other teachers recognize the relationship between aspects of their own behavior and the behavior of the students, and who can help them to set up learning experiences and environments for the enhancement of consciously selected objectives.

Mosher and Sprinthall (1971) have moved forward with an action program. Seeing no formal mechanism for "the deliberate development of positive psychological growth for all children in the school (p. 8)," they have set up a program sponsored jointly by the Harvard Graduate School of Education and the Newton (Massachusetts) Public School System: a curriculum development project to restructure the learning experience for secondary school students. The psychology of learning is basic in this project both in the pedagogical approach and for the attainment of desired objectives. A series of laboratories have been set up to refocus objectives away from the traditional content of psychology as an academic subject and toward psychology as a means of educating students in their own personal/psychological development. This project appears to be a significant step in the development of programs for the preparation of psychology teachers.

A second trend, observable in the Mosher and Sprinthall (1971) project and in other studies (Jones, 1968; Loevinger, 1970), is for experimentation and research in the application of learning theories to be carried out in schools and communities rather than under the controlled conditions of a university laboratory. Fieldwork involving systematic observation and other experimental methods is increasingly included as a part of the student's learning experience. It follows that the high school teacher of psychology should be familiar with such techniques and the facilitation of learning through field experience for the learner in high school as well as in undergraduate or graduate learning at the university.

Consideration for psychological values in educational

future-planning is another increasingly apparent trend. The title and selection of content for *The Seventieth Yearbook of the Society for the Study of Education, The curriculum: retrospect and prospect* furnishes evidence of this. Bruce Joyce (1971), for example, in his chapter on the curriculum worker of the future, expresses the opinion that "the great dynamic challenge of the future is to develop, in addition to more highly efficient structures for education, entirely new modes of education designed to help people create new solutions to problems and to define problems that were not perceived before (p. 311)." Joyce views as equally important, in a time when culture is growing stronger and more powerful and society is more urbanized and alienated, the production of humanistic modes of education. These modes would help people make contact with each other in new and stronger ways and can help individuals create lives which are unique, uniquely fulfilling and socially productive, even transcendentally cooperative.

If this vision of humanistic educational values and objectives is to be realized in practice, it will need teachers with a sound basis in the psychology of learning, including the social psychology of learning. It would require teachers prepared to develop and interpret the objectives of the curricula in the interaction of teachers and learners. Furthermore, teachers of psychology will be needed who will interact with teachers in other subject areas, with administrators and curricula developers, as well as with students, to achieve psychological learning objectives cutting across subject areas and age levels.

"Open education" in various forms (open corridor schools, schools without walls, learning in community settings) represents another attempt to realize psychological values in learning; values more openly assessed in relation to social goals and adult performance. So far many more diverse forms of learning experience seem to be apparent at the elementary level than at the secondary level. However, there are rapidly increasing numbers of variations appearing at the secondary level also, in both public and private schools; individual programming, independent study kits, modules, learning centers, mini-schools, "storefront" schools and schools like Harambee and Harlem Prep. Teachers need to be well grounded in the psychology of learning in order that the psychological values sought through these innovations can be realized. Students, too, will need to have greater knowledge of how to promote their own learning since the aim in most innovative approaches is to make the learner more responsible for his own learning. A brief overview of some of the premises and learning outcomes sought in open education is sufficient to illustrate the need for knowledge and skill in the creative application of learning psychology for both teachers and students. The following summation is drawn from the writings of Featherstone (1968, 1971), Rathbone (1971), Silberman (1970), and Weber (1971), and from numerous other reports as well as my own observations of innovative programs.

Some Premises and Learning Outcomes
Sought in Open Education

1. Individualization of learning: the fundamental independence of each learner, interacting with nearly any responsive element in his environment in a learning experience which is his alone.
2. Responsibility of the learner for his own learning: learning seen as a result of a child's own self-initiated interaction with the world.
3. Knowledge idiosyncratically formed: knowledge not inherently ordered or structured, nor automatically subdivided into various disciplines.

4. School learning environment modeling life outside the school: open education classrooms conceived as miniature models for an organically structured, dynamic, and flexible society; multiage grouping of older and younger children; peers, teachers, assistants, visitors intermingle in a community of learning.

5. Teaching viewed as a lateral interchange between two persons, one of whom happens to have a special need for something possessed by the other: student makes demands on the teacher rather than the opposite.

6. Psychoemotional climate planned to attain psychological values and objectives in learning: alleviation of the "pressure cooker" atmosphere with each child engaged in his own task de-emphasizing competition among peers; development of self-esteem with an attitude toward error which does not imply stupidity or inferiority; development of openness and trust in expression of feelings in which interpersonal defensiveness has nearly disappeared; implementation of the tenet stated in the Plowden Report (1967), that to live life fully as a child is the best preparation for adulthood.

7. Responsibility of the teacher to make any ethical or philosophical issues clear: no arbitrary division implied between moral and intellectual, such that children perceive school learning as properly intellectual, and moral issues are not to be discussed.

The fifth of the recent trends appears to be a growing realization of the implications of social anthropological studies for the psychology of learning. Recognition of the fact that a human being develops his human qualities through a cultural heritage, and that what and how we learn is shaped by the culture in which we learn (Benedict,

1934; Mead, 1955, 1966, 1968), combined with studies like Anne Anastasi's (1958, 1965, 1968) on psychological testing it has led, for example, to the concept of the culture-free test, since although no test can be totally culture-free or free of cultural bias. There seems to be a growing awareness that although our ways of living, our personalities and all our learnings are socially and culturally determined, we need not be prisoners of our society and culture. Social anthropology shows us that there are social and cultural alternatives, that man is highly flexible and capable of living in many other ways than those to which the people in any given society are accustomed.

This opens up the question of choice, which in turn poses the question of criteria for deciding the direction of social and cultural change and how it is to be accomplished. Consider the magnitude of the problem if we say, for example, the criterion to use in deciding on the direction of cultural or social evolution should be that of optimum development of the individual within society. Despite the magnitude and complexity of the problem of evaluating and deciding among alternative lines of action in relation to selected criteria, we perceive the possibility of controlling the direction of change. This means we perceive a responsibility for consciously deciding among alternatives including responsibility for choosing not to choose. A chapter entitled "Future-Planning as a Means of Shaping Educational Change," by Shane (1971) in the NSSE Yearbook provides an overview. A proliferation of studies in the 1960s explored directional alternatives under such titles as ORPHIC (Organized Projections of Hypotheses for Innovations in Curriculum), the RAND Long Range Forecast, "World of the Year 2000," Kahn and Wiener (1967), "Conceivable World of 2100," and "100 likely innovations," a list prepared by Kahn and Wiener

(1967), published in *Daedalus*; and later, Michael's *The Unprepared Society,* (1968), and Toffler's *Future Shock,* (1970).

It is the responsibility of the educational psychologist, the teacher of psychology and the psychology curriculum planner to deal with the psychological aspects of problems, in an interdisciplinary approach. In the context of the trend toward a search for a more humanistic society and human-centric education the psychology of learning will be more highly valued.

Shane (1971) observes that however traumatic it may be for man to be thrust into the terrain of an unfamiliar tomorrow with an unreliable map, the experience is also one of great potential promise, for both society as a whole and for educators. He believes that the promise of the present resides, at least in part, in the very rapidity of the changes that have unsettled the slower, evolutionary pace of less dynamic centuries. He is optimistic because he thinks the speed with which our lives are being altered suggests that more can be accomplished now in less time than ever before in history.

B. F. Skinner is a notable example of a learning psychologist who has enjoyed responding to the challenge with his *Walden Two* (1948), and his recent publication, *Beyond Human Freedom and Dignity* (1971). Skinner's proposal for control of social and cultural evolution through selective reinforcement is now a challenge to other learning psychologists either to join with him or to offer alternatives based on tested psychological theories of learning.

Last of the recent trends noted here is the recent advance in studies of cognitive and affective learning. The recent research and publications of Jerome Bruner (1966, 1968), Jean Piaget (1967, 1969) Ulric Neisser (1966),

David Ausubel (1965, 1968), Silvan Tomkins (1965) and Carroll Izard (1965) are some noteworthy examples.

CONTENT AND METHODS FOR TEACHER PREPARATION IN THE PSYCHOLOGY OF LEARNING

Content and methods appropriate for the preparation of high school teachers of psychology would follow guidelines drawn from the psychology of learning and development. One of these guidelines would provide increased flexibility in the selection and sequencing of content and more diverse methods of providing learning experiences. That there is no one monolithic body of knowledge that must or can be covered in a given area is certainly a view growing in acceptance. Accordingly, the criteria for selection of content are that it be meaningful and functional for the learner. Moreover, psychological studies of interaction between content and method imply that both be chosen in relation to the interest, needs, abilities, and background experience of the learner. Again, following psychological guidelines, methods of teacher training would include selection of a variety of learning experiences such as: laboratory experiences in schools and community environment; demonstration; films, lecture; discussion; improvisational drama; peer teaching; simulation studies; review of the literature on theory and research in aspects of learning relevant to problems or areas of interest; informal experimentation in the development of the learner's theories, explanations and interpretations of how he and others learn; and evaluation and measurement of learning outcomes with the use of feedback in future-planning.

SUMMARY

Recent trends in educational development provide evidence of the urgent need for teachers of psychology of learning at the secondary level. The broad scope and complexity of the problems, from changes involving specific behaviors of the individual learner to comprehensive future-planning for educational, social and cultural evolution, emphasizes the need for a thorough and meaningful preparation for the teacher and curriculum planner. As a member of the school community, as well as of the larger community, the teacher of psychology has the opportunity, as well as the obligation, to see that what we know about the psychology of learning is applied. Without it, the hard-won innovations of recent years will be lost, as many have been in the past, through misapplication by those whose enthusiasms were not supported by the necessary knowledge and skill. The areas in which competency is required include familiarity with research findings, theory and application in behavioral, gestalt and cognitive psychology, in the social psychology of learning, in special areas such as motivation and retention and in evaluation and measurement of learning outcomes.

REFERENCES

Anastasi, A. Heredity, environment and the question "how"? *Psychological Review,* 1958, 65, 197-208.

Anastasi, A. *Individual differences.* New York: Wiley, 1965.

Anastasi, A. *Psychological testing.* (3rd ed.) New York: Macmillan, 1968.

Anderson, R., & Ausubel, D. (Eds.) *Readings in the*

psychology of cognition. New York: Holt, Rinehart & Winston, 1965.

Ausubel, D. *Educational psychology: a cognitive view.* New York: Holt, Rinehart & Winston, 1968.

Benedict, R. *Patterns of culture.* New York: Mentor Books, 1934.

Bruner, J., Olver, R., & Greenfield, P. *Studies in cognitive growth.* New York: Wiley, 1966.

Bruner, J. *Toward a theory of instruction.* New York: Norton, 1968.

Coleman, J. *Equality of educational opportunity.* United States Department of Health, Education, and Welfare, Office of Education. Washington, D.C.: United states Government Printing Ofiice, 1966.

Cook, A., Mack, H., & Kernig, W. *The open school.* New York: Praeger, 1972.

Featherstone, J. Report analysis: Children and their primary schools. *Harvard Educational Review,* 1968, **38,** 2.

Featherstone, J. *Schools Where Children learn.* New York: Liveright, 1971.

Friedenberg, E. *Coming of age in America.* New York: Vantage Books, 1963.

Friedenberg, E. In Nordstrom, E., Friedenberg, E., & Gold, H. *Society's children.* New York: Random House, 1967.

Jackson, P. *Life in classrooms.* New York: Holt, Rinehart & Winston, 1968.

Jones, R. *Fantasy and feeling in education.* New York: Harper, 1968.

Joyce, B. the curriculum worker of the future. *The Seventieth Yearbook of the National Society for the Study of Education,* 1971, **I,** 307-355.

Kahn, H., & Wiener, A. The next thirty-three years: a framework for speculation. *Daedalus,* 1967, 705-732.

Kahn, H. & Wiener, A. *The year 2000.* New York: Macmillan, 1967.

Loevinger, J., Wessler, R., & Redmore, C. *Measuring ego development.* San Francisco: Jossey-Bass, 1970. 2 vols.

Mead, M., & Wolfenstein, M., (Eds.) *Childhood in contemporary cultures.* Chicago: University of Chicago Press, 1955.

Mead, M. *Continuities in cultural evolution.* New Haven: Yale University Press, 1966.

Mead, M. *Coming of age in Samoa.* New York: Morrow, 1968.

Michael, D. *The unprepared society: planning for a precarious future.* New York: Basic Books, 1968.

Mosher, R., & Sprinthall, N. Psychological education in secondary schools: A program to promote individual and human development. *American Psychologist,* 1970, 25(10), 911-24.

Mosher, R., & Sprinthall, N. Psychological education: a means to promote personal development during adolescence. *The Counseling Psychologist,* 1971, 2(4), 3-82.

Neisser, U. *Cognitive psychology.* New York: Appleton, 1966.

Piaget, J. *Six psychological studies.* New York: Random House, 1967.

Piaget, J., & Inhelder, B. *The psychology of the child.* New York: Basic Books, 1969.

Plowden Report. *Children and their primary schools.* A report of the Central Advisory Council for Education (England), Lady Plowden (Chairman), Vol. L: Report, Vol. 2: Research and Surveys. London: HMSO, 1967. (In United States, British Information Services, New York.)

Rathbone, C., (Ed.) *Open education: The informal classroom.* New York: Citation Press, 1971.

Shane, H. Future-planning as a means of shaping educational change. The curriculum: retrospect and prospect. *The Seventieth Yearbook of the National Society for the Study of Education,* 1971, I, 185-218.

Silberman, C. *Crisis in the classroom.* New York: Random House, 1970.

Skinner, B. *Walden two.* New York: Macmillan, 1948.

Skinner, B. *Beyond freedom and dignity.* New York: Alfred Knopf, 1971.

Skinner, B. *Cumulative Record.* New York: Appleton, 1972.

Sprinthall, N., & Mosher, R. *Studies of adolescents in the secondary school.* Harvard Graduate School of Education, Center for Research and Development, 1969. Monograph No. 6.

Toffler, A. *Future Shock.* New York: Doubleday, 1970.

Tomkins, S., & Izard, C. *Affect, cognition and personality.* New York: Springer, 1965.

Weber, L. *The English infant school and informal education.* Englewood Cliffs, New Jersey: Prentice-hall, 1971.

16. *Outline for a Program of Graduate Training of High School Psychology Teachers*

HARWOOD FISHER

RATIONAL OF THE PROPOSAL

This is a proposal for a planned sequence of post-master's courses and experiences to prepare teachers of psychology at pre-college levels, i.e., for elementary and secondary schools. The proposal is designed to provide thorough grounding in core areas of psychology as they relate to problems of teaching and learning. It is designed to accomplish the following specific training goals: (1) To provide well-trained teachers of psychology on a pre-college level, and (2) to train persons who can develop their own pre-college curricula in psychology. It is proposed that a coordinated offering be made available for licensed teachers who are teaching or are considering teaching pre-college psychology. A letter of completion will be issued.

The long-range goals include the following: (1) expanding the social science exposure of high school students in relevant directions; (2) creating new channels for vocational opportunity for teachers in the social sciences; and (3) providing foundations in the high schools for those students who will be future social scientists and psychologists.

There is at present an increase of interest in teaching social studies, although many teacher trainees who wish to go into history and related areas have not been able to find jobs. There is also a growing need for a channel for the adolescent's interest in social science, politics, sociology and related areas. It is envisioned that:

1. Creating new positions in teaching high school psychology will provide new vocational choices and opportunities for teachers interested in the social sciences.

2. The trend toward studies in sociology and student concern in this area needs to be supplemented by a careful psychological look at the individual's motives and the individual's determination of events around him.[1] Psychology courses for adolescents are socially and intellectually necessary.[2] The training of the high school psychology teacher should include preparation for dealing with the interpersonal relationships of adolescents

3. The interest of adolescent students in psychology will provide early direction for vocational development and choice.

According to Parrott 1970[3], 49 out of 50 states offer high school psychology. In California, according to Parrott, more than 60 percent of the high schools may be teaching psychology this year. Parrott concluded that

---

[1] G. Van Hooft, chief of Secondary Curriculum. Personal communication, 1971.

[2] Sprinthall, R. Symposium on Pre-College Psychology, APA Convention, Washington D. C., September 1971.

[3] Parrott, G. High school psychology exists. *Teaching of Psychology Newsletter.* December, 1970, 4.

many, if not most, high school psychology teachers would like assistance with their courses. Courses at present are being taught at four New York City high schools (public). In New York State, high school psychology is taught in 66 districts. The need to service the school and community and to create new jobs for the high school teacher interested in teaching social studies, indicate a clear demand for high school psychology.

The problem of proper teacher preparation is summed up by R. A. Goodale[4] who indicates that in a Pennsylvania survey, only about one-third of high school teachers of psychology had a course in experimental; that in a Michigan survey, only 4 out of 17 such teachers had *majored* in psychology; and that in a survey on western New York, *no* majors were found in a sample of 25. If psychology continues to be taught by inadequately prepared teachers using haphazard curricula, unnecessary confusions may arise, for both students and teachers. These would include the teacher's understanding of the student's self growth and his personal development, as well as a broad concept of the nature of psychology as an academic discipline.[5,6] A clear program setting adequate standards of preparation for the teacher of psychology in the secondary schools is necessary, and should probably be implemented by State and City certifications or licenses.

---

[4]R. A. Goodale. A survey of high school teachers of psychology in Massachusetts, *Teaching of Psychology Newsletter*, June, 1970, 7-8.

[5]Cf. Goodale, *op. cit.*

[6]Cf. R. G. Hunt, *et al.* Psychology in the secondary school curricula of western New York. *Teaching of Psychology Newsletter*, June, 1969, 4-6.

SUMMARY OF GOALS

1. To provide well-trained teachers of psychology on a pre-college level
2. To train people to develop pre-college curricula in psychology
3. To expand the social science offerings available to high school students
4. To create new channels for vocational opportunity in the social sciences
5. To provide foundations in the high schools for future social and behavioral scientists and psychologists.

SEQUENCE DESIGN

The post-master's sequence of courses is congruent with an individual approach to the training of our teachers. Current New York State certification includes the psychology teacher within the social science area. However, each social science teacher, in accordance with his job requirements and his interests, may need to specialize in a given area (psychology, sociology, economics, etc.)

A major purpose of the sequence is the development of proficiency in psychology and in the teaching of psychology on the high school level.

While the considerations here do not include certification they do concern the *preparation* of teachers.

The sequence described is consonant with Standard III A and III B (preparation in areas of individual interest) as set forth by the New York State Department of Education.[7]

[7]University of the State of New York. A new style of certification. Albany, New York, March 1971, 10.

The core course areas of the sequence are in accord with the concern of the standard of the New York State Education Department.

Course Areas

The major areas of educational psychology which offer special ways of understanding the teacher-learning process are:

A. Motivation (Individual Psychology)
B. Developmental Psychology
C. Social Psychology
D. Learning

Each of these areas offers a way of thinking about, understanding and approaching the problems of learning and teaching in the classroom. In addition to these four core Areas (A-D), all students will be provided with special courses in the teaching of psychology (E) and foundations courses designed to prepare them in measurement and research methodology (F).

This proposal builds a sequence around *core areas*. The general rationale for this approach is as follows:

1. Core content courses should provide a foundation in the ways to think about and ways to understand the teaching-learning process.

2. Each core area represents a way of understanding this process, and directs itself specifically to the literature in this connection.

3. The special area, principles of teaching psychology, is particularly necessary for the teacher who is working with adolescent students.

4. The high school teacher of psychology should not be isolated from other psychologists and should understand research methodology.

COURSE AREAS AND TITLES[8]

Area A — Individual Psychology

    Core course: Educational Psychology of Motivation
    Elective: Motivation: Thinking and Perception

Area B — Social Psychology

    Core course: Educational Social Psychology
    Electives: Attitude and Belief, Change in the Class-
             room
             Educational   Applications   of   Group
             Dynamics

Area C — Developmental Psychology

    Core course: Developmental Psychology in Educa-
             tion
    Electives: Developmental Psychology of Adoles-
             cence
             Developmental Patterns in Different Cul-
             tures
             (This elective is designed for development
             by the Department of Anthropology. The
             course would be co-taught by an anthro-
             pologist and psychologist.)

[8]The course titles included here are those available in the School of Education course sequence at City College, New York City. They are included here as specific examples of courses within core areas. It is recognized that individual schools would certainly need to vary these offerings in accordance with many local and internal considerations.

Area D — Learning

Core Course: Advanced Educational Psychology I
Electives: Advanced Educational Psychology II
            Computers in Education

Area E — Teaching of Psychology

Core course: Teaching of Psychology in the Second-
              ary School
              (This course is under development for
              adoption by the Department of Sec-
              ondary Education. The course would
              be co-taught by methods and founda-
              tions instructors.)
Electives: Independent Study and Research in an
              Academic Subject
              Teaching of Sex Education and Family
              Living
              (This course would be taught by the
              Department of Health and Physical Edu-
              cation, with a consultant from the Foun-
              dations Department.)

Area F — Measurement and Research[9]

Courses: Student in consultation with adviser may
          take two courses in this area. The *core*
          course will be selected on the basis of the
          student's background. Credit toward this
          requirement in Area F may be given for

[9] In practice, this flexible arrangement is very necessary. The backgrounds of teachers entering such programs is very varied, relative to specific courses.

certain courses taken on the graduate level in order that the student meet entrance conditions. The *core* area will be in either research *or* measurement depending on the student's background and needs.

Sample Area F Programs

Sample   One: Content Seminar in Psychological Foundations
Research Seminar

Sample   Two: Appraisal of Intelligence, Aptitude and Learning
Appraisal of Personality
Educational Measurements in the Secondary Schools

Sample Three: Descriptive Statistics in Education
Statistical Inference in Education

In Area F, if a student shows outstanding preparation, he may, in consultation with the adviser, elect a two-course sequence in advanced courses.

ENTRANCE REQUIREMENTS

1. Recognized Master's degree
2. Certified status as teacher or eligibility for such status
3. The following course equivalents (undergraduate or graduate)
   a. Introduction to Psychology
   b. Experimental Psychology
   c. Adjustment or Personality

d. Physiological Psychology
e. Introduction to Measurement
f. Introduction to Statistics

These last three courses (d,e,f) may be included within the program if there are enough elective credits available. (If the student has a strong background in some required course area and can be exempted from enough credits, he may substitute elective credit for the d,e,f courses.)

It is recognized that most applicants will not have majored in psychology. The candidate may present any 6 credits within the above and arrange with the adviser to take missing courses in A through D for undergraduate or graduate credit in the school of education or in the psychology department. An examination may be substituted for missing prerequisite courses. Students will technically maintain a nonmatriculated status.

OVERALL SEQUENCE CREDITS

In the post-master's sequence, the student *must* take:

1. The core course in each of the five areas (A through E) for a total of 15 credits.
2. In Areas A through D, the student takes one elective in each of three areas (9 credits). He may apply credit toward this requirement from the courses taken to meet entrance conditions.
3. In Area F, the student must take two additional courses under advisement (6 credits).
4. Total credits required: 30. (The adviser may, on the basis of the student's preparation require that the student take the Applied Statistics Laboratory along with the statistics courses.)

Part 4: Issues in Certification

17. *Certification Workshop:*
Summary and Analysis

WILLIAM SIVERS, Coordinator
JAMES M. JOHNSON, Editor

To date, the issue of certification for psychology is very confusing within state departments of education because psychology at the secondary level is a relatively new area of curriculum. Certification, therefore, is nonexistent in New York State for high school psychology teachers. This raises the questions: "Who is teaching existing psychology courses in high schools?" and "What are their qualifications?" The next obvious concern is what steps need to be taken to clarify the status of high school psychology curriculum and teachers.

These questions and concerns are a sample of the issues discussed during a panel workshop on certification of psychology teachers in New York State. The discussants and audience included representatives from the State Department of Education in Albany, New York, college personnel involved in training students interested in high school psychology, current school psychologists and current teachers of high school psychology.

It was quickly recognized that certification and curricu-

231

lum are interrelated in a number of ways. Both certification requirements and curriculum demands effect what a student will be exposed to in a psychology course; therefore, certification must deal with the problem of what teachers are offering in their psychology courses. As it exists now, many high school psychology programs or courses are taught by teachers not specifically trained in the teaching of high school psychology. In other words, psychology may be an extra course taught by a history or biology teacher. Often these teachers are qualified biology or history instructors but their background in psychology may not be adequate or may be too biased to be an adequate representation of the field of psychology. In such cases, the course content often tends to emphasize the area of abnormal psychology and mental hygiene. From the point of view of many psychologists and educators, high school psychology should not be restricted to this aspect of psychology. Rather the course content should deal with such areas as learning, motivation, human behavior, and experimental aspects of psychology which to most outside the field are unfamiliar disciplines within psychology. Therefore qualified teachers are needed to insure an appropriate curriculum in secondary psychology. Carefully defined certification standards can facilitate appropriate teacher training.

This problem of presenting a balanced curriculum in high school psychology is compounded by the inability of most schools to hire a teacher to teach only psychology since, in most schools, this does not involve a full-time teaching load. Therefore, in the past, most schools have been hiring teachers that can handle psychology in addition to another specialty area. Since this problem is mainly one of placement of qualified psychology teachers, it was suggested that certification of psychology teachers require exposure to a wider range of courses in order to insure a versatility in prospective secondary psychology teachers. Such suggestions led to the possibility of certification in social or behavioral sciences rather than in psychology alone so that teachers are qualified to teach a range of courses from psychology, sociology and anthropology. This plan would make it easier for academic administrators to hire someone with a broader base of certified skills. It was also thought that this plan would help to solve the problems of unqualified teachers in psychology and inappropriate or biased course content in these courses.

The above discussion led to the following questions: (1) Who should be certified to teach psychology, and (2) What should be the criteria for certification? The first question instigated a lengthy debate on the qualifications of school psychologists as teachers of psychology. Most everyone was in agreement that a strong background in psychology was necessary in order to insure that appropriate course content would be passed on to the students. It was agreed that school psychologists undoubtedly do have psychology exposure to some extent. Their background typically involves a baccalaureate and/or graduate degree in psychology, but it was questioned whether their approach to psychology would be too psychotherapeutic to be an adequate curriculum for high school psychology.

Another concern about such use of school psychologists was their education qualifications. No school psychologist undergoes student teaching as a requirement for their certification. The question remains whether they would be able to perform adequately as a teacher, even though they may be well qualified in terms of curriculum content. In response to this concern, it was mentioned that school psychologists are required to have an internship in the schools which might be equated to student teaching. The fact that the concerns during the school psychology internship are quite separate and more on an individual basis than the classroom and student contacts experienced during student teaching was taken into consideration.

An additional concern about the use of school psychologists for teaching psychology involved the current demands on their time. It was pointed out that in many areas in New York State, schools must share psychologists and such a situation would leave little or no time to teach a psychology course for one or two hours a day in any given school. The demands on their time for testing and counseling already exceeds the man-hours available.

As a point in favor of using school psychologists, it was stated that it might give them a more positive image among the teachers in the schools. As it stands now, very often school psychologists are viewed with suspicion and as being apart from the mainstream of the school activity. If they assume the role of teacher at least part time, this may help to bridge the gap between them and the teaching personnel which often exists. Countering this proposition, was the response that teaching might jeopardize the image of the school psychologist for the student. It was questioned whether the students might feel as free to consult about personal matters with someone they have had as a teacher.

The issues involving the use of school psychologists for teaching high school psychology courses was debated at length, and there was as much support for, as well as dissatisfaction with, the idea of a school psychologist in this capacity. Support rallied behind the fact that school psychologists would certainly have the knowledge of psychology that many present teachers do not have. The main point of dissatisfaction revolved around the probable deficiency of school psychologists in the area of teacher-training. It was pointed out that in New York State, since there is no certification standard in psychology, school psychologists would be able to teach psychology at least on a part-time basis. A suggestion was made that possibly school psychologists would be a temporary solution to present teaching problems of high school psychology and that, in the near future performance criteria and competencies could be set up for future training and certification programs in colleges and related institutions.

This temporary solution proposed about the use of school psychologists led to the next point of discussion, namely, the mechanics of certification. The key questions in this issue seem to be, (1) What should be the competency and/or performance criteria, and (2) Who should be the judge of these criteria? At present within New York State, the criteria problem has been relegated by the State Department of Education to the colleges and universities within the state. Individual colleges and universities have proposed specific teacher-training programs which are approved by the State Department of Education after their review and evaluation. Following this procedure, competencies are usually spelled out in terms of the completion of a certain number of courses and groups of courses. Following the completion of this prescribed sequence of courses, a degree and New York State certification would be awarded.

Another procedure for certification which might be considered and is currently getting some attention by the State Department of Education is individual certification based on performance competency. Within this procedure a person would be asked to demonstrate prescribed critical skills that are deemed related to teaching in a given discipline, and if these skills are adequately displayed, certification would be granted. This is an important break from the previous college training procedure in that there is no prerequisite college attendance required by this latter certification procedure. Theoretically a person may acquire the required competencies in discipline and teaching methodology by a wide variety of means, and then avail himself of the evaluation by the performance criteria of the State Education Department.

This second arrangement presumes that a set of specific behavioral performance criteria have been proposed and agreed to. We are certainly not at this stage of development at this time. Such a certification procedure presumes a clear statement of curriculum content for secondary psychology as well as mutual agreement on standards of teacher performance. The first concern reflects back to the problem of what kind of course will be taught at the high school level. Will there be only one course? Will the course have a different focus depending on whether the students are pre-college or terminal students? Is the high school psychology course for pre-college students to be viewed as a forerunner of the freshman general psychology course in colleges or should it be viewed as a possible replacement for such a course? It was cited that some colleges have complained about high school students coming into college psychology courses overconfident in their knowledge of psychology acquired in general freshman courses. In response to this it was stated that a number of colleges are utilizing advance placement tests which allow students with various high school experiences to skip over some of the freshman level courses, therefore reducing the possibility of redundancy and consequent motivational problems. Once again it appears obvious that the need for a concise objectively stated high school curriculum in psychology is imperative before many aspects of certification standards and even teacher training can be adequately developed.

The above discussion deserves some further editorial comment. Two issues which appear to be key aspects of the discussion were the curriculum training of the future psychology teacher and also the certification standards that might prevail for this discipline. Throughout the discussion it was repeatedly stated that the well-trained secondary psychology teacher should have a minimum of 18, 24 or 30 hours of undergraduate/graduate psychology hours. Frequently this type of training in psychology was equated to having a major in the discipline. I believe it is a faulty assumption to think that a specific number of course hours or a sequence of courses designed as a major are the appropriate or even desirable prerequisites for teaching psychology at the secondary level. Certainly some of the course content of advanced undergraduate courses for psychology majors cannot be seen as appropriate or even helpful ingredients for the high school psychology teacher. An alternative might be a sequence of related courses which expand on a wide range of basic principles of psychology in ways that will be appropriate, helpful and relevant to the adolescent student. For example, an undergraduate major course, theories of personality, may not be nearly as appropriate as an equally sophisticated course in personality development, which might emphasize the application of personality theories.

In terms of training and certifying new teachers for the growing need in high school psychology, the question of supply and demand is a critical one. For many school districts, a full-time psychology teacher is more supply than the current demand. One obvious answer to this is that we are in a period of growth within this academic discipline and that probably the student demand at the secondary level will increase in numbers and expand in courses with the result that a full-time person or persons for psychology might not be inappropriate. However, given the current situation, it appears academically appropriate to train secondary teachers for a broader range of behavioral science courses which might include psychology, sociology, anthropology, political science and maybe some aspects of economics. A training program at the State University of New York at Plattsburgh which is sponsored by the National Science Foundation is following this route in its training program.

Even when the student and course demand justifies the hiring of full-time psychology positions, the cross-discipline training approach has several advantages. Having teachers that are sensitive to the cross-discipline relationships should help to develop in the secondary students an appreciation for the interdependence of these behavioral sciences and to avoid the academic exclusion that usually occurs. Also, as the demand for personnel expands, it will be possible to develop departments of behavioral sciences within high schools. This will avoid the isolation of having the single psychology teacher and the single sociology teacher who have no specific departmental affiliation with their colleagues.

The extensive discussion about the current role of school psychologists and the possible use of them as part-time teachers seem to miss some key points. At times, it appeared that the major concern was developing a way which might better integrate the school psychologist into his school. This is not the primary purpose of the discussion or the workshop. The primary purpose is to establish a new area of curriculum, namely psychology and/or behavioral sciences in the high schools, and to pinpoint the training process to prepare excellent teachers for this new curriculum area. This is the primary objective and all other issues should be reviewed secondarily to this. Once these issues have been clarified, a more rational and calculated view of how the school psychologist may fit into this domain can then be undertaken. Once the specifics of adequate curriculum and training have been pinpointed there is always the very real possibility that not only school psychologists but also other current high school teachers may qualify for certification in this new discipline by an appraisal of their individual credentials or by the completion of an approved in-service training program focusing on this curriculum area.

18. Psychology in New York State High Schools

GORDON E. VAN HOOFT

I welcome this opportunity to review with you the current status of psychology courses in New York State high schools, some of the historical background of this development during the past several years, the nature of some of the courses of study we have reviewed, and some of the problems that have accompanied the introduction of these courses.

It is always gratifying to find that some of those who teach in colleges and universities are concerned about and interested in how they can help teachers in secondary schools who are attempting to add new dimensions to the curriculum. In fact, in many cases it is the students who are applying the pressure for new courses to help them cope with their problems. During the past 14 years since Sputnik, we have seen much curriculum activity that has involved cooperative efforts by college and high school

This paper was presented at the Symposium on Problems in High School Psychology, City College of the City University of New York, January 1972.

people. This effort has paid off in revised and improved offerings in many of the traditional curriculum areas and, in some cases, in new offerings. The developmental process has also had a payoff in building or strengthening ties between the schools and the colleges.

Let me add that I am presenting this brief report from the perspective of my previous position in the Education Department with responsibility for secondary curriculum development. I have had relatively little direct contact with programs in the schools except as locally developed courses of study have been submitted to the Department for approval. I have frequently discussed some of the problems with both field supervisors in our social studies and science offices and with Dr. William Sivers and others in our Bureau of School Psychological Services. Dr. Sivers has visited several schools at our request and has reviewed most of the proposed courses of study that we have received. I have leaned heavily on him for help because in general, our specialists in social studies and in science have not had sufficient educational or experiential background to provide all the expertise needed. From this perspective I approach my assignment on this panel.

THE STATUS OF PSYCHOLOGY COURSES

We do not have a State syllabus for a secondary level course in psychology as we do for courses such as economics, government, biology, chemistry, or other common elective offerings. Any school that offers psychology, therefore, must develop its own course of study. In some cases this takes the form of selecting a textbook to serve as the basis of the course. More generally, a teacher is asked to prepare a written course description for consideration by the school administration and approval by the local board of education. If credit is to be used toward a State diploma, the course description is submitted to the Department along with other data requested on the application form that indicates, among other things, the grade level at which it will be taught, the length of the course, the number of students and — most important — pertinent information about the teacher.

At the present time, we know of about 60 high schools in the State that are teaching some type of psychology course. Not all of these schools have submitted course descriptions for approval, but the pattern seems to be about the same. In general, most of the courses are offered as 20-week electives in grade 12, frequently to a single section. We do not have total enrollment figures, but obviously only a small fraction of the students in the 1274 public and nonpublic schools in the State are currently being involved.

Although our records are incomplete, only a handful of schools offered a psychology course before the mid-sixties. There has been a significant increase in the number of schools offering elective courses in social studies since the two-year American history course and Regents examination were discontinued as the new State social studies program was implemented. The freeing up of grade 12 for electives encouraged schools to offer economics, government, sociology, psychology, anthropology and other courses. We have developed syllabuses for economics and government because these are the two most common electives. Sociology is the next most popular elective with psychology close behind. But, the relatively small number of schools offering either sociology or psychology indicates that most schools have not voluntarily added these courses. With the worsening fiscal crisis, it becomes increasingly difficult for a school to offer elective courses to relatively small numbers of students. It is also correspondingly difficult for us to encourage schools to add a course to the program that requires additional local costs for staff, materials, etc. It becomes problematical, therefore, as to what will happen in the near future with respect to the number of schools that will add a psychology course to their curriculum. I assume that similar constraints will operate in other states, compounded by problems related to course development, teacher training, and teacher certification. Perhaps the cooperative efforts implied by this Symposium will alleviate some of these problems and permit the growth to continue.

THE NATURE OF THE COURSES

I am appending to this report some typical course outlines in the barest of detail. As you examine these, you will see several common topics in the general psychology courses. In addition to a common treatment of psychology as a science, you will see a focus on growth and development, patterns of behavior, learning, mental health and interpersonal relations. Two of the outlines are for social psychology courses which are less common than the more general introductory course.

"The courses range from content courses about psychology (experiments, research, theories) to reviewing problems in human relations and personality with a focus on the student (his problems and relationships). In years past, Dr. Sivers usually resisted the latter and endorsed the former. During the few years he has come to move toward support of the latter beacuse of student activism and demands for relevance.

Our primary concern is whether or not the typical school

situation is able to incorporate this newness without harmful backlash. Boards of education, school administrators, and parents need to be brought into, and to understand clearly the mechanics of what is going on in, the more 'humanistic courses.' A primary problem has been the qualifications of the teacher. Virtually, there are none in terms of regulations, except that he be certified to teach something.

Dr. Sivers has both witnessed and experienced courses with a humanistic approach. Most are well done by sensitive people. While competency in psychology is required, this does not have to be equated precisely with being a licensed psychologist or a certificated school psychologist. People with majors in psychology or others may display unusual competency, particularly in the area of human relations and sensitivity.

We believe that the 'teachable moment' for some aspects of values and humanistic education is a junior and senior high school.[1] Many of the questions of humanistic psychology have been shunned traditionally by the schools in terms of their willingness to underwrite intensive personal evaluation of one's values."

I have not attempted to make a careful analysis of all of the course descriptions that we have on file. As Dr. Harwood Fisher noted when he reviewed a few of these with me in Albany recently, considerable insight can be gained about the nature of current offerings from a sample of these locally developed courses.

In passing, I should note that there seemed to be much more interest some years ago in focusing on abnormal behavior than in recent courses we have reviewed. In general, this was also true of the so-called problems courses offered in grade 12 in social studies during the 1950s. To a generalist, it appears that there is a focus now more on the knowledge and skills that will help students to cope with

---

[1] *Editor's note:* Compare the statement here with Dr. Roen's in Chapter 7 concerning research findings relative to "natural curriculum."

the problems they face — understanding themselves, relating to their peers, coping with drugs, etc.

I shall leave further analysis to those of you in the discipline. However the analysis needs to be made in the context of the total curriculum — especially in view of the recent emphasis on the process goals in science teaching and on inquiry and concept development in social studies. Those who will be taking psychology courses in high schools in the 1970s will have been exposed to both the processes and tools of the scientist — whether it's been in the areas of physical science, biological science or social science. You also need to be aware of the fact that many of the basic facts, understandings, skills, and tools associated with the discipline of psychology are permeating more and more of the health education courses that are now mandated in New York at both the junior and senior high school level. The implications of these developments for those interested in strengthening the teaching of psychology are evident. Any course developed as an elective must build on and extend concepts that have already been introduced at earlier levels in different curriculum areas especially in science, health, social studies, and also home economics. No course should be frozen into or need to be based upon a single textbook. Students need to be exposed to, and given some opportunity to make use of, the methods and tools of psychological investigation. In short, the course should neither be book-centered or teacher-centered, making this a real challenge for those psychology professors who themselves operate in the lecture mode.

SOME PROBLEMS PECULIAR TO INTRODUCING PSYCHOLOGY INTO THE CURRICULUM

As revealed in some of the course descriptions that we

have reviewed, it is apparent that the course content is far too extensive to be presented in anything other than a cursory fashion, largely through lecture, in the time allocated. In a few cases, deficiencies have been noted that represent obvious errors or misconceptions on the part of the teacher who developed the course of study. Often, topics are introduced that obviously require prior knowledge that cannot be assumed on the part of the student who may reach incomplete or even wrong conclusions. Frequently, the course description reveals inadequacies on the part of the teacher in using the methods and tools of the psychologist, which generally leave little of the aspects of psychology as a science.

Much of this, of course, reflects the obvious fact that some of the teachers are very poorly prepared to teach a course in psychology. Observations in the classroom by Dr. Sivers, members of his staff, and others have confirmed that many teachers who have been observed are presenting misconceptions and getting involved in some topics where they cannot cope with the questions that students have. Generally, such teachers have had a minimal background by way of specific courses in the field.

For this reason, we have requested additional information as to the background of the teacher who has been assigned to teach a course submitted for approval. Such approval is contingent on evidence that the teacher has some depth and breadth in undergraduate and/or graduate courses in psychology. With the lack of specific certification requirements, we have felt that this step has provided some protection for the students. It does not necessarily follow that a trained school psychologist will do a good job in the classroom, and a few courses developed by such staff members have also been deficient. In several instances, the school psychologist has been involved in the development of the course and has been a key resource person to back up the teacher in the classroom.

SOME FINAL OBSERVATIONS

In the post-Sputnik period, psychologists have been increasingly involved in the various national projects in most of the curriculum areas. This involvement has proven to be most valuable. At the present time, I see two major points of entry where psychologists can help in secondary schools. One is a very essential role in developing health education materials, not only in the area that we have labeled as Strand III, Mental Health, in our State program, but also in more effective approaches to tackling the sociological health problems in Strand II, dealing with the areas of smoking, drugs, and alcohol. The second area is the specific need for developing a model course of study for psychology that would reflect the best practices of curriculum design, teaching strategies, student activities and evaluative devices.

If this Symposium can lead to some cooperative action, it will have served a useful purpose. I have appreciated this opportunity to share some ideas with you and will welcome any opportunity to cooperate with any future activity or project that emerges.

Appendix A. High Schools in New York State Offering Psychology Elective Courses 1970-1971

Akron Junior-Senior High School
47 Bloomingdale Avenue
Akron,New York   14001

Beaver River Central
Beaver Falls, New York   13305

Bennett High School
2885 Main Street
Buffalo, New York   14214

Brighton Central School
Monroe and Elmwood Ave.
Rochester, New York   14618

Brushton Moira Junior-Senior
  High School
Gale Road
Brushton, New York   12916

Canandaigua Academy
Granger Street
Canandaigua, New York   14424

Canarsie High School
1600 Roackaway Pky.
Brooklyn, New York   11236

Clarence Senior High School
9625 Main Street
Clarence, New York   14031

Cleveland Hill Senior
  High School
Mapleview Drive
Cheektowaga, New York   14225

Cold Spring Harbor High School
Turkey Lane
Cold Spring Harbor, New York
  11724

East Rockaway Junior-Senior
  High School
Ocean Ave.
East Rockaway, New York   11518

East Syracuse Minoa Central
  High School
Fremont at Kirkville
East Syracuse, New York   13057

Elizabethtown Lewis Central
  School
Court Street
Elizabethtown, New York   12932

Elmont Memorial Junior-Senior
  High School
555 Ridge Road
Elmont, New York   11003

Forestville Central High School
Academy Street
Forestville, New York   14062

John H. Glenn High School
330 Cuba Hill Road
Huntington, New York   11743

Herricks Senior High School
Shelter Rock Road
New Hyde Park, New York
   11040

Highland Falls Junior-Senior
   High School
Mountain Avenue
Highland Falls, New York
   10928

Homer Senior High School
80 South West Street
Homer, New York   13077

Ithaca Senior High School
N. Cayuga Street
Ithaca, New York   14850

Johnson City High School
435 Main Street
Johnson City, New York   13790

John F. Kennedy High School
Kennedy Drive
Plainview, New York   11803

Kendall Junior—Senior High School
   High School
S. Main Street
Kendall, New York   14476

Keshegua Junior-Senior
   High School
Nunda, New York   14517

Kings Park High School
Route 25A
Kings Park, New York   11754

Lockport Senior High school
250 Lincoln Avenue
Lockport, New York   14094

Maine Endwell Central School
712 Farm to Market Road
Endwell, New York   13760

Ward Melville Senior High School
Old Town Road
East Setauket, New York   11730

Middletown Senior High School
Grand Avenue
Middletown, New York   10940

Monroe Woodbury Senior
   High School
Route 32
Central Valley, New York   109

Morris Central School
Morris, New York   13808

New Berlin Junior-School
   High School
17 Main Street
New Berlin, New York   13411

New Rochelle Senior High School
265 Clove Road
New Rochelle, New York   10804

Oceanside Senior High School
Brower and Skillman Avenue
Oceanside, New York   11572

Olean Senior High School
410 W. Sullivan Street
Olean, New York   14760

Ossinging Senior High School
29 S. Highland Ave.
Ossining, New York   10562

Pelham Public Schools
17 Franklin Pl.
Pelham, New York   10803

Riverhead Senior High School
300 Pulaski Street
Riverhead, New York   11901

Franklin D. Roosevelt Senior
  High School
South Cross Rd.
Hyde Park, New York   12538

Schoharie High School
Main Street
Schoharie, New York   12157

Paul D. Schreiber Senior
  High School
101 Campus Drive
Port Washington, New York   11

Sleepy Hollow High School
210 N. Braodway
N. Tarrytown, New York   10591

Southampton Senior High School
70 Seland Lane
Southhampton, New York   11968
  11968

Southold School
Oaklawn Avenue
Southold, New York   11971

Stamford Central School
1 River Street
Stamford, New York   12167

Suffern Senior High School
Hemion Road
Suffern, New York   10901

Tuckahoe Junior-Senior
  High School
65 Siwanoy Blvd.
Eastchester, New York   10707

E.L. Vandermeulen High School
Old Post Road
Port Jefferson, New York
  11777

Warsaw Junion-Senior High
  School
Warsaw, New York

Westfield Junior-Senior
  High School
Main Street
Westfield, New York   11787

Westhill Junior-Senior
  High School
4501 Onondaga Blvd.
Syracuse, New York   13219

Whitehall Junior-Senior
  High School
Buckley Road
Whitehall, New York   12887

Williamsville Senior
  High School (North)
1595 Hopkins Road
Williamsville, New York   14221

Others

Rhodes School
11 West 54th Street
New York, New York   10019

South Lewis Junior-Senior
  High School
Turin, New York   13473

Added in 1971

Bethlehem Central School
Van Dyke Road
Delmar, New York   12054

Penfield Central School
Scribner Road
Penfield, New York   14526

Pine Bush Central School
Pine Bush, New York   12566

Walt Whitman High School
31 Walt Whitman Road
Huntington Station, New York
   11746

Appendix B. Major Topics
in Representative Psychology Courses
on File in the Bureau of
Secondary Curriculum Development, NYSED

Walt Whitman High School, Huntington Station (1971)
— Social Psychology (20 weeks)
  • Social Psychology as a Behavorial Science
  • Learning
  • Social Adjustment
  • Small Group Interaction
  • Interaction in Society

Pine Bush (1971)
— Psychology (20 weeks)
  • The Field of Psychology
  • The Human Organism
  • Growth and Development
  • Motivation and Emotion
  • Perception
  • Learning and Thinking
  • Individuality and Personality
  • Conflict, Adjustment and Mental Health

Bethlehem Central School, Delmar (1971)
— Psychology (20 weeks)
- Introduction to Psychology
- Understanding Human Behavior
- Patterns of Behavior
- Mental Health
- Interpersonal Relations
- Psychology of Learning
- Employment and Job Satisfaction

Greene Central School (1965)
— Social Psychology (Man and Society) (40 weeks)
  I Individual Man (20 weeks)
- How Man Studies Man
- Uniqueness of Individual Behavior
- The Driving Force in Man's Behavior
- Language Controls Man's Behavior
- Culture Influences Man's Behavior
  II Man in Groups (20 weeks)
- Man Behaves in Groups
- Leadership
- Fate of the Individual in the Group

Tuckahoe (1968)
— Psychology (20 weeks)
- Psychology as a Science
- Learning
- Intelligence
- Personality
- Response to Conflict and Frustration
- Abnormal Behavior

19. Some Procedures of Certification Relative to Initiating a Secondary Education Program in Psychology

SISTER MARY TALBOT KELIHER, I.H.M.

The class of 1970 of Marywood College expressed interest in teaching. Several surveyed their home districts and states; little encouragement was obtained. Faculty members pro-proposed further investigation for two reasons. Unqualified teachers had been asked to teach psychology (APA indicated at least 9,000 had only an average of *five* undergraduate credits in psychology); and the possibility of part-time teaching to help defray graduate expenses would justify the initiation of a teacher-training program. A proposal was prepared to submit to evaluators. A description of the proposal, its rationale and some results of a survey conducted now follows:

PROPOSAL

It is proposed that Program I (psychology majors) be expanded to include secondary education requirements

Portions of this material were presented and discussed at the Symposium on Problems in High School Psychology, New York, City University, January 1972. The proposal was first put forth November 1970.

thus enabling students to teach psychology at the secondary level.

The Marywood undergraduate psychology faculty has recognized the necessity of training teachers of psychology. At the graduate level Plan II is designed to prepare students for the teaching of psychology in high schools and colleges.

RATIONALE

The undergraduate faculty has considered this proposal for two reasons:

1. During the past few years an alarming number of school districts have introduced psychology into the high school curriculum. In many instances already overburdened and ill-prepared teachers have accepted the assignment.
2. Since many of our graduates are financially unable to pursue graduates studies immediately, the possibility of teaching psychology part-time would afford opportunity for financial income and enable the student to share and impart theoretical principles.

RESEARCH

To validate the initiation of a secondary education program within the psychology department, a consideration of the research by Noland (1966)[1] was made by the faculty. Accordingly, a survey of state certification bureaus and the local school districts was made.

RESULTS OF OUR SURVEY – FALL 1970

Thirty-eight state boards of education responded to the questionnaire presented at the end of this paper.

[1] See the review by Fisher, Gray, and Weiss, Chapter 1B.

Twenty-one states believe a certification program is valuable, while ten do not; seven did not respond to this question. Eighteen states believe a certification program is needed; sixteen of these states already have a certification program. The sixteen states are

Alabama	Kansas	Mississippi	Utah
Alaska	Kentucky	Montana	West Virginia
Arizona	Michigan	New Hampshire	Wisconsin
California	Minnesota	New Mexico	Wyoming

In many cases the certification was a social science combination.[2]

Only one state has a curriculum for the teaching of psychology at the secondary level. The majority do not believe a curriculum is necessary. In nine states the majority of school districts include psychology in the program. Most replies indicated that if psychology is taught it should be elected by or required of only seniors or advanced students.

The following fifteen states appended comments and certification requirements to their replies:

Arkansas	Montana	South Carolina
California	New Hampshire	Vermont
Illinois	New Mexico	West Virginia
Louisiana	Ohio	Wisconsin
Mississippi	Oklahoma	Wyoming

The local school districts responded immediately. Of Lackawanna County's school districts, nine responded to the questionnaire. At present psychology is offered or

[2]See the paper by G. Van Hooft, Chapter 18.

about to be offered in five districts; one school has a qualified teacher. Each of these districts would accept student teachers from our program. Within the local diocesan school district only one Catholic high school offers psychology. A part-time qualified teacher of psychology and history is employed at this school.

Present research supports the previous national surveys. Local reports indicate the rapid growth the field is enjoying and offer possible teacher-training opportunities. The proposed curriculum at Marywood College is in agreement with Noland's critique that the teacher should have a major in the field.

In February 1971 the Clearinghouse on Precollege Psychology conducted a survey of state psychological associations which indicated that Iowa has submitted recommendations to their state department. In January 1972 Ohio will begin granting certification in social psychology.

The State of Pennsylvania has granted Marywood permission to initiate a teacher-training program. The certificate will be in Comprehensive Social Studies indicating that the individual is a major in psychology with competencies in allied areas. At Marywood the secondary teacher of psychology is a major with at least 36 credits in psychology, 18 in education and with electives in other social sciences. Local school districts are slowly initiating high school courses in psychology and sociology. Recent student teachers taught both areas. State officials are quite reluctant to develop a separate certificate as they believe administrators could not employ a full-time psychology teacher in most areas within the state.

The requirement that the student be a psychology major was determined from a review of the literature and recommendations of the Division on Teaching Psychology of APA, and to enable the student to qualify for graduate school.

Since our initial brief survey local changes have occurred rapidly in the following respects:

1. The county schools were just beginning to offer psychology in 1970; the program has since developed considerably. Marywood students have opportunity for teaching experience within several schools of the newly formed Intermediate Unit #19 (three county area). Statistics are not available on the present status of psychology, but I was recently invited to speak as a consultant to the Instructional Planning Council (comprising twenty School Districts) on the formulation of psychology curricula.

2. Formerly, only one Catholic high school within the local diocese offered psychology; presently, six consolidated schools include psychology in the curriculum.

3. Only two Marywood majors elected the teaching of psychology at the secondary level in the class of 1971; six elected it in the class of 1972; four in the class of 1973 and nine in the class of 1974. Subsequent classes are growing in number as knowledge and interest broadens.

4. Whereas graduate students were offered this possibility, many were not directly concerned or knowledgeable regarding the status or need for secondary teachers. Now, teachers certified in other areas are investigating the possibility of certification in psychology.

5. It may have appeared in October 1970 that the Pennsylvania Board of Education did not believe that a demand for psychology in the secondary schools would become an issue. However, several colleagues in different teacher-training colleges have been refer-

red to investigate Marywood's program. I would still prefer, and will continue working for, certification in psychology, per se.

6. Recently the Philadelphia Society of Clinical Psychologists expressed an interest in the teaching of psychology in high schools; specifically, in the prerequisites, training, and standards of existing programs.

7. Although the state of Nevada did not respond in 1970, a Marywood student just completed a month of observation and expects to return to Las Vegas in September 1973 to fulfill her student teacher requirements. Every high school in Las Vegas has a fine psychology program. Students from other colleges were also involved in field experiences within this school district.

QUESTIONNAIRE SENT TO
TEACHER CERTIFICATION BUREAUS

1. Do you believe that a certification program for teachers of psychology at the secondary level is valuable?
    _____ Yes _____ No
    If so, why?

2. Do you believe that a certification program for teachers of psychology at the secondary level is needed?
    _____ Yes _____ No
    If not, why not?

3. Does the state of _____ have such a certification program? _____ Yes _____ No
    If so, what are the basic requirements?

4. Is there a state curriculum for the teaching of psychology at the secondary level? _____ Yes _____No
   If yes, would it be possible to obtain a copy? _____Yes
   _____ No

5. Do many of your school districts include psychology in their program? _____Yes   _____No

6. If psychology is taught at the secondary level, do you think it should be
   _____required of seniors
   _____elected only by seniors
   _____ required or elected only by advanced students

                                                    Thank you.

Please use back of page for additional comments.

Part 5: Funded Programs

---

20. *Workshop on Funding Programs: Summary and Analysis*

JAMES M. JOHNSON
Coordinator and Editor

With increasing frequency psychology is becoming part of high school curricula. As this interest in psychology as part of high school curricula grows, it is becoming obvious that there are two main areas of concern. The first is the development of adequate curriculum for high school psychology, and the second, the preparation of teachers who are specifically qualified to teach psychology and related courses. It became obvious in the discussion involving high school and college personnel that these two issues cannot be tackled in isolation of each other. There are problems facing each of these areas of development which are mutually related.

It was expressed that a careful exploration of key issues and objectives within secondary psychology curriculum development and teacher training should occur before a proposal for support could be adequately generated. In order to generate an adequate proposal, there should be a clear statement of purposes and objectives for the experi-

263

mental program. Most funding agencies will look very critically for the inclusion of such statements. Once the objectives have been stated, the procedures to implement them should be delineated. It is generally realized that when an experimental program is being proposed, the procedures cannot be rigidly fixed. They certainly should remain responsive to findings that evolve as the program progresses. It was readily agreed among the discussants that some statement and plan for evaluation is a critical part of any proposal.

Evaluation has consistently been a difficult area in teacher-training and curriculum development; however, funding agencies insist that the project directors give attention to, and make some attempt at, systematic evaluation of the proposed program. The expected results of such evaluation will be a statement of procedures that were effective in establishing a viable program and how they were effective in achieving the goals of the program.

A final area of concern among funding agencies is the generality of the results of the experimental program. Many funding agencies view their role as providing support to selected institutions to try programs with the result that a product will emerge that can be adopted in a wide range of similar institutions. It is assumed that with the grant monies available, the project will be successful at the host institution. The more critical question is whether the program can be implemented at this institution and similar institutions within the normal framework of operations and budget. It is only under these conditions that the program has any chance of successful adoption.

As was mentioned earlier, the two major concerns within pre-college psychology are teacher training and curriculum development. The discussants thought that a cooperative program between several colleges and high schools would be desirable. It was considered that the colleges could provide the leadership, coordination and background in the discipline and training models. The high schools were viewed as providing the physical plant, a student body to work with, as well as very important teacher inputs and information about the culture of the high school environment.

Another question raised regarding teacher training was whether it should focus on preservice training or in-service training. There was some discussion that training for high school psychology is more than just acquiring competency in another discipline area. It also seems to be an appropriate time to review in critical detail the procedures in teacher training. The current trends and pressures to review teacher training in the light of skill competencies and performance criteria should be reviewed as any new training program is developed. For these reasons it appears that a preservice experience is probably most desirable in filling the need for high school psychology teachers. It is obvious that if cooperative programs as described above are to occur, any preservice program will have definite ingredients of in-service training as a variety of practicums are carried out in local schools. The current teachers in the schools would certainly be involved in these practica and would hopefully derive some benefit in terms of professional training.

The above discussion led into the question about whether the teacher training should be concerned more with methodology of teaching or with content of the discipline within which the teacher would be working. There was some feeling that teacher-training programs should concentrate on teaching methodology, and that concern for discipline content should be viewed as a secondary issue. The teacher is seen as picking up his competency in the discipline quite separately from the methods of teaching experiences. There is probably some strong support for this position when teacher-training is viewed in relation to many subject disciplines, such as the natural sciences. The relationship between training methodology and these disciplines is not readily apparent. Some discussants felt that in the case of psychology and the behavioral sciences there are strong possibilities for overlap and integration between the two training aspects. An additional point regarding these two training aspects might be mentioned editorially; it appears that teacher-training in psychology, and more generally in the behavioral sciences, has a unique opportunity to combine the two. Certainly psychology and sociology have a great deal to tell us about the underlying theories and processes of learning which we are looking at in the classroom, the dynamics of groups which we are looking at in the classroom, and the development and maturational stages of adolescence which we would be seeing in the secondary classroom. Each of these issues are of vital concern in methodology programs and also add to the repertoire of content information of the high school and/or behavioral science teacher. It does appear that the psychology/behavioral science high school teacher has the unique opportunity to combine his discipline training with his methodology training.

The concern about the relationship between teacher training and discipline content led to the next discussion about programs for curriculum development. It had been mentioned earlier that these two areas of activity were related by several mutual concerns. If there is to be a close connection in training between methodology and discipline, then obviously a program must be sensitive to any curricula which may emerge for secondary psychology. It was pointed out that before any curriculum project can be undertaken, several key questions must be answered. The first question is whether psychology should be viewed as an elective course for the pre-college student, or whether it should be geared to the needs of the students who might be terminating their formal education at the high school level. A followup question to this concerns the type of psychology content and experiences to which the high school students should be exposed. Another point to be considered is whether there should be more than one course in psychology available to the high school students, and if so what the definition of each should be. It was mentioned that a number of surveys have been and are currently under way to assess teacher and student attitudes toward the content of high school psychology courses. Also, the American Psychological Association is coordinating the most comprehensive curriculum project for secondary psychology. This organization has assumed the responsibility to organize the administrative and program structure for the curriculum project and to seek out possible sources of funding.

After discussing some of the aspects of projects that are needed for high school psychology, a general discussion followed about the steps to be taken in developing a proposal. This discussion may be summarized by listing a series of general guidelines. First, the person or persons interested in such a project should carefully set out the purposes and objectives of the project. Second, the person initiating the idea should seek out other interested personnel at his institution or related institutions. If it is to be a cooperative proposal, the personnel should include both high school and college personnel. Third, the group that evolves from these contacts should read the information available from funding agencies and select the sections within these agencies that are compatible with the purposes and goals of their program. Fourth, an initial contact with the funding agency should be made by way of a letter of intent to apply for the grant. This letter of intent should be addressed to the designated person for the particular section of the agency and will serve as an introduction of the institution proposing the grant to the funding agency. Fifth, following the letter of intent and followup communication, a completed proposal should be drafted with the guidance of the personnel from the funding agency. Sixth, during the review period between submission of the official proposal and allocation of funds, the project directors should prepare the home institution/institutions for implementation of the proposed project.

Following the listing of these guidelines a discussion of possible funding agencies took place. On the federal level the agencies that appear best suited for this type of proposal are the National Science Foundation, the Office of Education, the National Institute of Education and the National Institute of Mental Health. These agencies would probably be most interested in pilot projects that have wide application following the experimental period. At the more local level, probably the best initial contact would be the state and local Boards of Education. For some institutions with selected populations or geographic locations, it would be wise to check the availability of funds under various title programs. These programs are usually geared for specific purposes and are less concerned about the generality of findings and information.

Following this discussion there are several editorial comments that might be added. The first is that in one of the current training programs for secondary behavioral science teachers, extensive use is being made of high schools and high school personnel. This gets back to the issue of whether a training program should be one of preservice or in-service. The training program referred to at the State University of New York at Plattsburgh is designated as a preservice program, but in the ongoing operations, there is extensive contact with high school teaching personnel. This includes the opportunity for them to have a variety of in-service training experiences. There are also summer workshops on teaching which are a combination of pre- and in-service training.

A final comment might be made about the organization of a grant proposal. When all the objectives of a program are set out and procedures developed, the resulting package is often so comprehensive and broad in scope that it requires a very large budget. Sometimes, the mere size of the proposed budget is a determining factor in not funding a project. An alternative to the procedure of submitting one large comprehensive proposal is to analyze the overall program and break it down into component parts which might then be submitted as smaller projects to a number of different funding agencies. In this way the dollar commitment by any one agency is not as large and if all components are funded, the program can still be carried out as proposed. Another advantage of obtaining funds from a number of different funding agencies is that the project is less dependent on the fiscal status of any one agency.

21. A Model of a
Training Program
for Secondary Behavioral Science Teachers

JAMES M. JOHNSON

A training program for secondary behavioral science teachers has been initiated at the State University of New York at Plattsburgh. This program is funded by the National Science Foundation under its Undergraduate Pre-Service Teacher Education Program (UPSTEP), and it is operating in conjunction with the previously existing program on this campus in the biological sciences. In awarding the initial funds for a proposed five-year program, the National Science Foundation noted that the behavioral science program at Plattsburgh is the first of its kind in the nation sponsored by NSF.

The intent of the program is to provide the secondary behavioral science education major with special exposure to a variety of classroom and practicum experiences in psychology, sociology and anthropology so that he approaches his teaching career with not only a technical knowledge of behavioral science phenomena but also some firsthand experiences in the actual research, conceptual and field experiences of a practicing behavioral scientist.

There are several concurrent strings of evidence that

This paper was presented at the symposium on Problems in High School Psychology, City College of the City University of New York, January, 1972.

indicate a pressing and immediate need for such a training program. A quick review of the recent surveys completed on the number of behavioral science courses being offered on the secondary level, and the level of preparation of the teachers handling those courses reveals two points. The first is that an increasing number of schools are offering at least senior electives in one or more of the behavioral science areas. Typically these offerings involve more than one class section of a specific discipline. What might be a typical example of this point is reflected in the community surrounding the Plattsburgh campus. During the first year of our program, three of the local high schools were offering one or more sections of behavioral science courses. These offerings involved five teachers. During the second and current year, the number of schools offering behavioral science courses has increased to seven and the number of teachers involved has increased to twelve. The reliability of this finding across a number of surveys makes this trend unmistakably obvious. The second finding of many of the surveys is that the formal preparation of the current teachers for teaching a behavioral science course is severely lacking. This deficiency in training is borne out by the statements of many of the teachers involved and also by recording and reviewing their academic preparation in subject areas allied to the behavioral sciences (Abrams & Stanley, 1967; Goodale, 1970; Hunt, et al., 1969; and Schumacher, 1972).

The situation just cited becomes even more dramatic and relevant to the New York geographic area when the action of the New York State Department of Education is reviewed. The new syllabus in social studies of the State of New York which was developed in the 1960s is now the official syllabus for the public schools. This changes the curriculum in social studies from a predominantly history-oriented curriculum to one strongly recommending instruction in specialized courses in behavioral sciences, specifically psychology, anthropology, sociology, economics and political science. (Social Studies Curriculum, 1967). The move to implement these recommendations has been considerably slowed by the lack of adequately trained manpower to properly implement the recommendations. This means that many of our teacher training programs continue to produce a now dated model of the social studies teacher.

Therefore one of the major goals of this training program is to develop a model training program which will adequately prepare students for this emerging new role of secondary behavioral science teacher. However, rather than just turning out another type of teacher with competencies in a given set of disciplines, we also want to take this opportunity to look very carefully at the general process of teacher education. One of the key ingredients in current teacher training programs which appears in need of modification is the level of participation by the teacher in their specific training discipline. The philosophy and experiences of the biological sciences training program on this campus have certainly reinforced this notion (Perkins, 1969). Essentially, we are saying that we want these teacher trainees to be research participants in their discipline rather than simply communicators of information about the discipline. The rationale for this position is that if the teachers are trained in the research and methodological skills of their discipline, they will be able to keep themselves current with the discipline for a considerably longer period of time than if they are simply trained to know the current information available in the discipline. In this age of rapid flow and turnover of information in both the sciences and social sciences, the obsolescence of the teacher by means of dated information is certainly a common and prevalent pitfall. A teacher who has been trained as a participant in his discipline should more readily be able to avoid this common plight.

To achieve the multiple goals mentioned above, there will be considerable emphasis on the following types of activities:

1. Teaching experiences at both the secondary and college level beginning in the teacher trainee's freshman year.
2. Research associateships with faculty members involved in on-going projects in the behavioral sciences and related areas.
3. Summer activities for the students ranging from field and research experiences in their institution to independent study activity which might extend work in areas initially contacted during the academic year to intensive workshops involving both project trainees and full-time public school teachers currently teaching one of the behavioral sciences.
4. Analyses of educational methods and formats for curriculum design, as well as reviews of recent trends in research in the behavioral sciences will be deliberately emphasized aspects of the entire program.

Next we should turn to consideration of some of the specific structures and technical aspects of the training program. The program is scheduled for five years duration. The objective is to recruit students as incoming freshmen and to follow them through in the training program until they have completed a master's degree in secondary education. By the end of the five-year sequence, it is expected that the first group of students will have obtained the B.S. degree, the M.S. degree and permanent New York State Certification. The proposal allows for approximately seven students to be recruited into the program each year. The five-year duration of the grant will allow a complete cycle for the first group of students recruited into the program. It is anticipated that the model which has evolved as a result of the experiences in the program will be incorporated as part of the regular curriculum of behavioral science secondary education at Plattsburgh. Therefore our goal during the five years of the program will be to implement and evaluate a number of different possible activities for a training program. Those components which appear to have yielded the best results will be retained and incorporated into the final model.

It can be readily seen, therefore, that the five years of the program will be a period of flux. At this point, I can relate some of the procedures that have been tried and give a preliminary report of outcomes.

One of the first concerns of the program was the recruitment of appropriate students. There are several current factors which require this part of the program to have very careful and extensive planning. First of all, New York State certification standards are set for secondary social studies programs only. These are programs in the traditional social studies format emphasizing history and geography. (While there have been some moves away from this format even at the level of curriculum design, the corresponding move on the part of teacher education programs and certification standards has not been equally rapid. A model for assessing trial projects in teacher education has recently been developed by the State Education Department and this may give some latitude to certification standards (State Education Department, 1971). Since there is currently an apparent overabundance of secondary social studies teachers, many graduating high school students are being dissuaded by their guidance counselors from entering secondary social science programs in their college curriculums; therefore such candidates constitute a dwindling population. Most entering college freshmen are unaware of the possibilities of teacher training which emphasizes the behavioral science disciplines. Given these conditions, we have found it necessary to notify liberal arts behavioral science majors as well as declared secondary social science majors in our recruitment process. In tapping this source of students, we have found a great number of students interested in the behavioral sciences and particularly in teaching these disciplines, but who are unaware of any program to accommodate their particular interest. The fact that many of the students that are recruited for the program have declared themselves initially as liberal arts majors reinforces the notion of the program that we aim to have these teacher trainees be specialists in their discipline and not people who view the role of an educator as simply a communicator of information.

It was stated in the initial project proposal that considerable attention would be given to criteria for the selection of students for the program. Of course, one of the best ways to validate a selection criteria is to review the credentials of those students who prove to be successful in the program. Since this is still a fairly new program, it would be premature for us to speak about the students' success in the overall program. At this time, however, we can indicate those factors which have been given some weight in the student selection process. The three factors which have been reviewed most carefully have been (1) high school performance, (2) expressed interest in teaching, particularly in the behavioral sciences and (3) ability to interact well interpersonally. As can be seen, previous academic achievement accounts for only about one-third of the decision. The remaining two elements in the decision process are carefully weighed during an interview. Of course, judgments on the basis of interview are liable to all the usual measurement problems. However, we can note that we have found high reliability among the judgments of up to four people participating in the interview of any one candidate. During the second year of the program, the recruitment interviews have included student participants as well as the project coordinators.

There have been a number of activities which the students have shared as common activities within the program. One of these has been assisting in the instruction of a section of general psychology at the Plattsburgh campus. We have developed a program at Plattsburgh in which we make extensive use of student instructors in the general psychology course (Johnson, 1970). This experience usually occurs in the second half of the student's freshman year or first part of their sophomore year right after they have taken the general psychology course. This experience, as it is designed, allows them to get an initial contact with the teaching process, and also exposes them to a variety of teaching strategies. This instructional experience is under the careful supervision of two of the staff members of the Department of Psychology at Plattsburgh.

Another major ingredient of the program which is started in the students' very first semester of involvement is their participation in one of the local high schools at least one half day per week. In this participation the students usually function first in the role of observer and then later as a general assistant to the course giving demonstrations, preparing small laboratory exercises and presenting lectures on particular topics. To prepare the students for their high school observations, they are given a number of presentations by Plattsburgh faculty about techniques to analyze the classroom process. These techniques allow the students to objectively quantify behavior patterns in the classes and to pinpoint the roles of the teacher and of the students. The observation analyses done in classes are exchanged among the group and discussed in order to reinforce the students' abilities to use these techniques of recording. If a student is asked by the cooperating high school teacher to give a demonstration or present a lecture, the teacher is asked to make the request sufficiently in advance so as to allow the student adequate opportunity to thoroughly prepare for this project. During this preparation stage, the student usually consults with the project coordinator about the available materials to use and techniques that might assure a worthwhile presentation. After each week's high school participation, the students are asked to submit a report about their observations and/or activites in the class for that week. These reports are submitted to a fellow student for review and reactions and then are submitted to the coordinator to read. The reports are returned to the students within a week and become part of the permanent file that each student is keeping on his high school activities.

In addition to the weekly reports, there are two other mechansims for getting feedback about the high school practicum experiences. The first way is by visits by the project coordinator to the various high schools in which the students are participating. During these visits which occur about every three to four weeks, the coordinator speaks with each of the cooperating teachers and reviews the activities of the student participant in recent weeks. Besides rendering information about the high school experiences, these visits by the coordinator have been found to have a number of other advantages. One of these distinct advantages is that it reinforces for the cooperating teacher the feeling that they are definitely involved in an ongoing viable program. The visits also allow sufficient opportunity for the teacher to air any questions or difficulties they might have concerning the student's participation in his class. This avoids the development of a difficult situation which might arise when ambiguity has been allowed to continue.

The second additional mechanism for obtaining feedback is through joint meetings that are occasionally held on campus for both the participating teachers and students. These meetings usually focus on a specific topic of concern in the secondary education setting. The result is usually a fairly free and open discussion about the total picture of high school education and not a restricted view of a single classroom setting. This type of meeting has been started only recently and is not without its difficulties. A major concern is the time and availability of the cooperating high school teachers. For this reason the meetings are necessarily infrequent and attendance by the teachers is variable. However the results of the initial efforts have been positive enough to warrant some continued effort along these lines.

As can be readily observed, the weekly high school participation is viewed as one of the critical key elements in our training program. We have found that it allows the students, very early in their careers, to answer some questions they might have had about teaching as a profession. These firsthand experiences either strongly reinforce their initial decision toward teaching or allow them to reevaluate this decision very early in their academic preparation. If their initial decision is reinforced and they reaffirm their decision in favor of teaching, these high school participation experiences allow them to share in the classroom process in a way that is typically reserved for the senior year student teaching experience.

Since so much emphasis is placed on these high school experiences, the role of the cooperating teacher is critically important. We attempt, as far as possible, to recruit teachers who are currently instructing in the behavioral sciences. But, more importantly, we are also interested in recruiting teachers who are interested in the overall goals of this program and not ones who view the students as just another student observation practicum. For these reasons we try to maintain some continuity of cooperating teachers from year to year and also strive to involve the high school teachers in the full range of the program-related activities. One of the mechanisms used to enhance the amount of involvement by the cooperating teacher is to give them the status of adjunct faculty at the college at Plattsburgh. As adjunct faculty members, they are entitled to a number of privileges in the use of campus facilities.

Another type of event which occurs fairly frequently as part of the program activities is a presentation by one of the college faculty members, a visiting consultant or one of the students in the project. These presentations usually focus on the person's research or practicum work in an area which is of interest to the group. The purpose of these presentations is to inform and update the participants about the information in a specific area of the behavioral sciences. The presentations are usually followed by a discussion period which allows exchange of opinions and an opportunity to look at the problem from a number of perspectives. These meetings are scheduled approximately every three weeks.

Another major common experience for all participants in the program is the summer workshop that is scheduled for each summer during the program. An attempt is being made to have these workshops as a combination of preservice and in-service training which would accommodate both the teacher trainees in the program as well as selected high school teachers from both the surrounding area and other geographic locales. The focus of the workshops has been on problems which are common to the wide variety of secondary education settings. Rather than setting up the usual student-teacher dichotomy, the attempt in the worskshop is to use each person participating as a resource for some aspect of the workshop. We feel that the experiences of each of the participants will allow them to make a productive contribution to the progress of the workshop. For example, this coming summer we plan to have an intensive exposure and evaluation of curriculum materials available for secondary behavioral sciences. Although there will be some faculty members involved in the organization and a few consultants to lend direction to the workshop, it is felt that the participating high school teachers will be able to provide a wealth of information about the problems in using various available materials. The students in the program on the other hand should be able to provide some information about means for evaluating the effectiveness of given types of materials and also describe alternative methods for using the materials. Our experiences in the workshop last summer have indicated that a structure which allows each person to be individually active appears to be more productive toward the learning experience than the workshop structure in which participants are asked to absorb information from experts.

Another experience which each student has during the summer is directed toward furthering one of the basic goals of the program, that is, extensive involvement in research activities of the behavioral science disciplines. For

10 weeks of the summer, each student is involved in a research practicum with one or more faculty members. This practicum may take place in a laboratory on campus or in a field setting, and may involve experiences ranging from basic animal research to field survey work. The goal of this summer experience is at least twofold: (1) it will develop the students' sensitivities to the fine points of research methodology, and (2) it will provide an opportunity for them to become quite expert in the research literature within a given area. There is also extensive opportunity available during the summer for the students to exchange with each other the kinds of experiences they are having in their research practicum. This type of dialogue should broaden their base of information about various kinds of methods and techniques that might be used in research programs.

Many of the activities and experiences we have been talking about so far have been aimed at revising the model of teacher education in general, that is, establishing a set of experiences which might result in better teachers whether they are behavioral science teachers, science teachers or humanities teachers. However, since the major portion of our mission is also to develop a model for a new type of teacher, namely, the behavioral science teacher, we are also giving very careful attention to developing a curriculum which might serve as a model undergraduate program for training such a teacher. Since it would probably be a faulty assumption to think that the courses being currently offered at our college could be rearranged in a new combination to produce an effective curriculum, we are urging the student participants in this experimental program to design specific activities and experiences which they feel would be productive toward their goal. It is our hope that with direction the students will set up sequences of experiences that systematically build on each other toward the terminal goal. The result of this sort of thinking so far has been that many of the students have taken extensive independent study work. To assure that the students maintain some continuity in their program of activities and do not fall into the trap of tacking together a series of discrete interesting experiences, each student is assigned to a three-man advisory committee. This committee has representatives from at least two of the behavioral science disciplines as well as one from education. Their role is to bring to the student information about the needs of the professional behavioral science educator. As the program progresses, we will constantly evaluate the effectiveness of the various kinds of experiences that the students design for themselves. Those that appear to have a commonly beneficial effect will probably become a formalized part of the training program. Hopefully by the end of our five years of experimental procedures we will be able to pinpoint a fairly specific, yet flexible, training model.

The need for our concern about curriculum at the college level is obvious. However we must also be quite concerned about the curriculum needs and demands at the secondary level. The curriculum structure of the secondary level will have a necessary impact on the program design at the college level. Since these two concerns are relatively inseparable we have been focusing our energies on both of them. In an attempt to obtain systematic and relatively complete information about behavioral science curriculums at the secondary level, the student participants in this program have designed a project for a survey of such curriculums in New York State. This project will be carried out during the summer of 1972 and the next academic year. The concerns of the proposal cover both the current offerings in behavioral sciences in New York State, the adequacy of these offerings as perceived by both students and teachers, and the level of preparation of the teachers involved in these courses. This concern with current standards of curriculum is congruent with the activities of the American Psychological Association. The APA is planning extensive activity along the lines of both survey work and curriculum development. It is interesting to note that the APA, which represents a single discipline within the behavioral sciences, is convinced that the appropriate first step would be toward the development of a general based curriculum in the behavioral sciences rather than a single discipline orientation.

A final focus of concern during the course of the program will be a review of current certification standards for secondary teaching. Although this is not a primary ingredient of the initial proposal, the activity of the project certainly puts the participants in the middle of these questions. It appears that the several growth factors in terms of number of courses in behavioral sciences being offered and the diversity of curriculums that will be developed over the next few years all point to the need for some review and probable revision of the certification standards for social studies teachers. A profitable starting point might be to review the experiences of other states along these lines and see what steps have been taken by these states to answer their particular needs. The information obtained from the student survey mentioned above will also be invaluable in providing an indication of the level of current involvement of secondary schools in the behavioral sciences.

Although the activities of the program are currently focused on many different directions, we see this as the luxury of having an experimental period. It is felt that there is a common thread which ties most of these activities together and that the results will take the form of a reasonably cohesive package. Of course the overall goal of this experimental period is that a workable model will be established which will be implemented at the Plattsburgh campus and hopefully other campuses for the effective training of the secondary behavioral science teacher.

REFERENCES

Abrams, A. M. & Stanley, J. C. Preparation of high school psychology teachers by colleges. *American Psychologist,* 1967, 22, 166-169.

Goodale, R. A. A survey of high school teachers of psychology in Massachusetts. *Teaching of Psychology Newsletter,* 1970, (June), 7-8.

Hunt, R. G., Bodin, A. M., Patti, J. & Rookey, E. Psychology in the secondary school curricula of western New York. *Teaching of Psychology Newsletter,* 1969, (June), 4-6.

Johnson, J. M. An experimental design for a General Psychology course. *Social Sciences,* 1970, 3, 35-43.

Perkins, H. J. Research: Key to learning and teaching. *Commission on Undergraduate Education in the Biological Sciences,* 1969, 5, 1-3.

Schumacher, G. Survey of psychology in Ohio High Schools. *Periodically,* 1972, 2, 1.

University of the State of New York, The State Education Department, Bureau of Secondary Curriculum Development, *Social Studies Curriculum,* Albany, New York, 1967.

University of the State of New York, The State Education Department, Bureau of Secondary Curriculum Development, *A New Style of Certification,* Albany, New York, 1971.

Index

APA
   "Behavioral Science
      Teacher", 47
   Committee on High School
      Psychology, 33
   Division on the Teaching
      of Psychology, 33
   Education and Training Board
      Committee, 31, 33
   "People Watching", 47
   "Periodically", 47
   recommendations of, 35
   role in high school
      psychology, 37-9, 47
   standardized course develop-
      ment plan, 12
Abnormal psychology,
   as a high school subject,
      134, 139-40
Abrams, A.M. and Stanley, J.C.,
      31, 40, 273, 287
Adler, A., 127
American Psychological
      Association, see APA
Anastasi, A., 213, 216
Anthropology,
   in the elementary
      grades, 125
Australia, 29
Ausubel, D., 215, 217

Behavioral sciences,
   in high school curriculum,

      124-7, 272-3, 283-4
   student interest in, *xii*
   see also under specific
      Subjects: anthropology,
      psychology etc.
Behavioral science teacher,
   model training program for
      271-86
Benedict, R., 212-13, 217
*Beyond Human Freedom and
      Dignity*, 214, 219
Boring, Edwin, 8
Brown, M., 124, 179, 206-19
Bruner, J., 125, 148, 182,
      183, 214, 217

California, 10, 46, 222
Canada, 29
Carey, Sister H., 123, 127-33,
      146
Certification,
   based on performance
      competency, 235-6
      in New York, 6, 201,
         231-61
      in Nevada, 260
      in Ohio, 259
      in Pennsylvania, 257-
         8, 259-60
   perspectives on, 231-9
   present state approaches to,
      257-60

procedures related to
psychology, 255-61
recommendations for, 113-14,
115, 231-2, 274-5
Chapko, M.K., and Fuchs,
A.F., 46, 55
City College of New York,
graduate and undergraduate
education, 16
Coffield, K.E. and Engle, T.L.,
25, 41
Coleman, J., 208, 217
College psychology teachers
attitudes toward high school
psychology courses, 12
lack of consensus among, 11
topics emphasized, 11
Culture-pair test, 213

Educational innovation, 208-16
Educational psychology, 198
*Elementary Psychology, or the
First Principles of
Mental and Moral
Science for High, Nor-
mal, and Other Second-
ary Schools and For
Private Reading*, 25
Elementary and junior high
school students, 126-7
Elements of Mental Philosophy,
24
*Elements of The Philosophy of
Mind Applied to The
Development of Thought
and Feeiings*, 25
Encounter group, in the
classroom, 6, 140, 200
England, *see* Great Britain
Engle, T.L., 15, 19, 23-43

Engle, T.L., and Bunch, M.E.,
26, 41
Erikson, E., 126, 127, 180

*Fantasy and Feeling in
Education*, 183, 185
Featherstone, J., 211, 217
Fisher, H., *xi-xiv*, 3-22, 120,
191, 221-9
Florida, 95-6
France, 29
Freedom To Learn, 182
Freud Sigmund, 8, 126, 127, 131
Friedenburg, E.Z., 181, 185,
208, 217
Funding programs
guidelines for, 267-8, 269
see also Workshops

Gallis, V.A., 123-4, 133-40
George, R.C., 141-2, 148
Gnagey, W.J., 57, 94
Goodale, R.A., 13, 15, 21, 223,
272, 286
Graduate training program,
objectives of 221-4,
proposed outline for pre-
college level psy-
chology teachers, 221-9
sequence design of courses,
224-9
see also high school
psychology teachers
Gray, Susan, 10-22
Great Britain, teacher
attitude, 28-9
Gwynn, J.M. and Chase, J.B.,
147, 148

Hansen, J.H., 12, 21
Heath, D.H., 183, 185

Helfant, K., 27, 42
High school education, 12
High school psychology teacher,
  academic preparation of 4,
      12-13, 15-18, 30-1,
      35-6, 46-7, 57-8, 70-83,
      86, 90-3, 96-8, 191-229,
      237-8, 255, 263-6, 268-9
  as therapist, 133-40, 160, 164
  attitudes of, 12, 28-9,
      100, 121
  characteristics of, 13, 15,
      61-4, 66, 70-90, 96,
      98, 102-3
  doctoral program for, 203
  functions of, 207-8
  Great Britain, 28-9
  institute attendance, 84
  lack of consensus
      among, 11, 155
  making referrals, 164-5
  Michigan, 13
  New York, 6-7
  objectives of, 5, 11, 32
  Ohio, 12-13
  Oregon, 11
  Pennsylvania, 13
  professional journals sub-
      scribed to or read, 84
  professional organizations
      a member of, 83-4
  professional responsibilities
      other than teaching, 29,
      61-3, 85
  topics emphasized, 6, 32,
      68-70, 86, 99-100
  see also teaching high school
      psychology
High School psychology
  programs,
  course characteristics, 6,
      12-13, 57, 65-70, 86,
      99-100, 104-5, 181, 244-
      6, 267
  curriculum development, 17,
      45-55, 92, 103, 123-48,
      209-10, 231-2, 246-7,
      248, 263, 264, 266-7
  factors inhibiting growth of,
      36-7
  history of, 25, 26, 104-5
  incidence of (domestic),
      California, 10, 46, 222
      Florida, 95-6
      Maine, 46
      New York, 10, 221-54
      Ohio, 46
      South Carolina, 11, 46
  incidence of (foreign),
      Australia, 29
      Canada, 29
      France, 29
      Great Britain, 28
      Japan, 30
      West Germany, 30
      Sweden, 29
  laboratory work, 199-200
  objectives of, 6-8, 10-14, 142,
      143-4, 155-8
  personality course, 127-33
  survey of, upper midwest and
      summer institute sample,
      57-94
      Florida, 95-112
  syllabus, 149-51

High school psychology student,
  attitude towards subject, 100
  characteristics of, 27-9
  grade level of, 98-9
  field work by, 149-54
  interest, 3-4, 7, 174, 198

needs of, 3-4, 7, 18, 113,
    114, 211
Hunt et al., 147, 148, 272, 286

*I Never Promised You A Rose
    Garden,* 128
Inhelder, B. and Piaget, J.,
    4, 21
Instructional material, 100,
    101-2, 128
    see also textbooks
Izard, C., 215

Jackson, P., 208, 217
James, W., 26
Japan, 30
Johnson, J.M., 20, 120, 121,
    231-9, 263-86
Jones, R., 183, 186, 209, 218
Joyce, B., 210, 217

Kasschau, R., 7, 11, 13, 19-20,
    21, 44-55
Kaufman, J., 121
Keliher, Sister M.T., 20, 120,
    255-61
Kenniston, K., 181, 186
Kirby, R.J., 29, 42
Kleitman, N., 45, 55
Klingelhofer, E.L., 48, 55
Kremer, R.J., 11, 15, 21

Laing, R.D., 128
Learning,
    cognitive and affective,
        214-15
Leeper, R.Q. and Madison, P.,
    182, 186
Living Psychology, 128
Loevinger, J., 209, 218
Louttit, C.M., 25, 42
Lipton, Ira, 149-54

Maine, 46
Markman, B., 53
Maslow, A., 127, 131
May, R., 128
McNeely, P.R., 11, 12, 22
Mead, M., 213, 218
Menges, R.J., and Trumpeter,
    P.W., 52, 55
Merrifield, P.R. and Schoeppe, A.,
    140, 148
Miller, Margaret, 7, 159, 173-86,
    187
Morris, J.A., 48, 50, 55
Mosher, R. and Sprinthall, N.,
    208, 218

Nebergall, N.S., 10, 13, 22
Neisser, V., 214, 218
New York, 6, 7, 10, 221-54
Noland, R.L., 11, 12, 13, 15,
    22, 256

Oberlin College,
    recommendations by,
        research team, 12
Ohio, 46
"Open education", 210-12
Oregon, 11

Parrott, G.L., 10, 222-3
Parrott, G.L., and Setz, G.,
    46, 55, 57, 85, 94
Pennsylvania, 13
"Periodically", 120
Perkins, H.J., 273, 286
Piaget, J., 4, 8, 21, 214, 218
*Practical Psychology: Human
    Nature in Every-
    day Life,* 24, 42
Pre-college psychology,
    see high school psychology

Psychology, *see* under specific
    headings, *i.e.* high
    school psychology
*Psychology: Its Principles and
    Application,* 101
*Psychology: The Science of
    Behavior,* 101

Rathbone, C., 211, 218
Relevance of Education, 183, 185
Robach, A.A., 24, 26
Robinson, E.S., 24, 42
Roen, S., 123, 124-7, 132, 147
Rogers, C., 127, 128, 182, 185
*Rudimentary Psychology for
    Schools and Colleges,* 25
Ryan, J.J., 20, 47, 57-94,
    145-6, 148

Scarf, M., 140
Schachtel, E., 8
Schoeppe, A., 120, 123-148
School psychologist, as teacher
    of high school psy-
    chology, 233-5, 238-9,
    247-8
Schumacher, G.M., 46, 55, 272, 286
Science curriculum, 49
Scribner, H., 20, 113-15
Sensitivity training, 137, 140,
    200
Shane, H., 208, 213, 214, 219
Silberman, C., 211, 219
Sivers, O.W., 231, 242, 245
Skinner, B.F., 127, 214, 219
Social studies teacher, as
    psychology teacher, 8, 30,
    86-9, 191-2, 193,
    certification of, 284
South Carolina, 11, 46
Sprinthall, N., 179

Stahl, R.J. and Casteel, J.D.,
    20, 95-112
Sweden, 29

Taba, H., 147, 148
Tanner, L.N., 49-50, 55
Teaching high school psychology,
    approach,
    experiential, 179-88
    experimental, 133-40
    field, 149-54, 164
    humanistic or human
        relations, 15-16, 28,
        29, 30, 114, 145, 210
    interdisciplinary,
        52, 214
    mental health, 33-5, 40,
        142-3, 155-6
    reinforcement, 175-8,
        187-8
    scientific component 16,
        28, 34, 35, 142, 143,
        155-6
    attitude of educators toward,
        12
    communication with students,
        159-89
    ethical considerations, 133-6
    objectives of, 5, 174
    problems in, 4-9, 145-6, 182
    recommendations for, 13-14,
        113-15

Textbooks,
    analysis of, 25-6, 32, 86
    assigned to students, 67-8,
        101, 128, 146, 151
    early publications, 24-5,
    need for, 13

Thornton, B.M., 10, 11, 13, 21,
    57, 94

Thornton, B.M. and Williams,
    B.J., 57, 67, 94
Tomkins, S., 215, 219
*Toward Understanding Human
    Personalities*, 182-3, 185

United Nations School, 7

Van Hooft, G.E., 20, 241-54

Walden Two, 214, 219
Watley, D.J., and Nichols, R.C.,
    49, 55

Weber, L., 211, 219
Weiss, Alfred, 121, 159, 160,
    179-86, 187
Weiss, Ethel, 10-22, 120, 144,
    155-71, 191-205
Westby, G., 28, 43
Workshops,
    intro. to, 119-22
    curriculum, 123-48
    funding programs, 263-9
    teacher training, 191-205

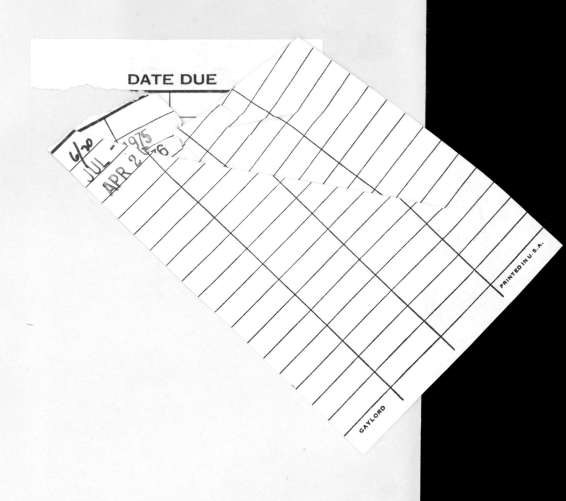

DATE DUE

6/20
JUL - 1975
APR 2 ? ?6

GAYLORD

PRINTED IN U.S.A.